GRATEFUL

By Eric Bischoff, with Guy Evans

ISBN-13 (Paperback Edition): 979-8-218-09178-1
ISBN-13 (Hardcover Edition): 979-8-218-09179-8
Also available in E-book (Amazon Kindle) format

For Loree, Garett and Montanna

Contents

GRATEFUL

All Possibilities

1

Albuquerque, N.M., March 2016: I'm sitting in the back of a pickup truck in the parking lot of the Westside Community Center, waiting to make my appearance on an independent wrestling show. It took me about eight hours to drive here, but with only minutes to go before showtime, I'll be damned if anybody sees me now. To the promoter of tonight's event, I have repeated my feelings ad nauseum: *just keep this thing a secret.*

Don't tell anyone who doesn't need to know.

It's hard not to smile back here. The assembled crowd – perhaps a few hundred of them in total – clearly don't suspect a thing. As they excitedly file into the venue, it looks like some of the performers in tonight's show have blended in with them. The very idea of a similar scene occurring elsewhere – prior to an episode of WWE's *Monday Night Raw*, for example – makes my smile even wider.

One thing is for sure - the contrast between the two worlds is fascinating. This small venue – likely one of the more, ahem, *affordable* settings that the *Destiny Wrestling Organization* could get a hold of – doesn't have any of the trappings of a major arena. In fact, it's situated in an area that would never be confused with other, more affluent parts of town – and that's being kind.

Still, I'm here, and not by necessity, by the way – I'm here by choice.

Sitting in my truck, I think back to an event produced under *entirely* different circumstances; specifically, my on-screen debut with WWE, the industry leader, televised to millions some 14 years earlier. On that night, the reaction to my surprise appearance – immortalized forever on WWE television – would become almost as famous as the appearance itself. Memorably, and shockingly, it was Vince McMahon himself - once my bitter business rival during the previous decade – with whom I embraced on the stage at Continental Airlines Arena.

That rumbling beneath your feet, I told Vince as 17,000 fans became unglued, *is a whole lot of people turning over in their graves.*

My agreement then to sign with Vince, the Chairman and driving force of WWE, sent shockwaves throughout the entire wrestling world. What followed, for yours truly, was an improbable - almost impossible, really – three-and-a-half-year run as *Raw*'s on-screen 'General Manager' (before wrestling's 'authority figure' role became, well, such an *agonizing* trope).

Quite naturally, back then in 2002, my decision to sign with Vince came with a simple request: *just keep this thing a secret.* Imagine that! I even took the liberty of flying myself in for that particular show, booking my own hotel, and doing everything possible to keep my presence under wraps.

And you know what? It worked.

Why did it work? It worked because the element of *surprise* is one of the most undervalued aspects of professional wrestling. Had I been advertised – had people known I was there – the audience still would have reacted, but the response would have been exponentially

2

weaker. I can't explain it - it's just *different* when you walk out, unadvertised, unexpected, and all of a sudden, there you are on a live wrestling show.

But here on this night – right now in Albuquerque - the final few patrons are starting to shuffle in. I could be wrong, but it looks like one guy may have spotted me in my truck. I see him slowly turn back to enter the building, and that's enough for me - the time to wait is over. I glance left, glimpse right, and soon make an immediate beeline for the backdoor entrance.

One step inside, and my grin is incandescent: *I'm in*.

As I approach backstage in this very small building, there's not a familiar face in sight. Rather, I'm greeted by perhaps 30 or 40 guys and girls – the wrestlers on tonight's card - most of whom are in complete disbelief at my presence. It's clear that the promoter has kept his word.

I can see now that my instincts were right. The promoter was respectful, polite and *painfully* honest during the initial contact - especially with respect to what his organization is trying to accomplish. Besides, if I'm to be candid, I always did have a soft spot for people just like him – young entrepreneurs, or people who are very passionate about what they're doing.

He realized that asking me here (via Twitter, no less!) was a long shot, but I thought, 'You know what? This guy is trying. He's hustling. He's passionate.'

I kind of shrugged and said, 'Here's my phone number – feel free to give me a call.'

3

All in all, it could certainly be described as an atypical situation – in fact, things couldn't actually be more different than what I'm used to. For the purpose of this show, I sense that some of the participants are here purely for fun, with only a few harboring greater ambitions. Of the latter category, it remains to be seen who will pan out. But taking in the entire group, one can see all kinds of potential outcomes.

All kinds of possibilities.

The enthusiasm surrounding my arrival is dying down now, at least for a second, as the wrestlers start laying out their matches, preparing the show in earnest. I find myself standing back, quite a bit away from everyone, as if to survey the scene from a distance.

It's fun to watch everybody get ready. It's fun to simply take in the moment, as I see so much of what I used to love – so much of my own early days in wrestling.

And just like that, that's how it hits me: I'm seeing the journey – maybe *my* journey – from the start all over again.

I know, I know. There are those of you screaming at this book already: *Eric! Enough of the sentimental crap!*

After all, this is 'Eazy E', *mucker futhers* - the man who changed professional wrestling with World Championship Wrestling, the nWo and Monday Nitro in particular. Chances are, you remember me not as the guy who surprised 250 fans in New Mexico, but rather the guy who reinvented the entire pro wrestling format!

4

In reading my opening salvo here, you may also be reminded of my previous book, *Controversy Creates Cash*, which began with a recounting of my WWE debut, and covered my entire career up until 2006.

I was very proud of that book, which debuted at #16 on the New York Times Best Seller list. I remember ending the manuscript in a very deliberate (and provocative) manner:

When people ask, 'Do you think there'll be another competitor to the WWE?' my answer is, 'I don't think so.' When people ask, 'Will you ever go head-to-head with Vince McMahon again?' my answer is, 'Probably not.'

But never say never.

In this business, you never want to *fully* close the door behind you. Then again, in all honesty, if you were to talk to me in 2006 or 2007, I fully believed that my days in pro wrestling were behind me. If you had asked me what the next 15 years of my life would look like, it would be *nothing* like what ultimately transpired.

Truthfully, over these past 15 years - while I've had some wonderful successes - I've had some spectacular failures, too. I guess it's a consequence of my nature. I'm often so, so right about things, but I've been pretty wrong about some things - as many fans can surely attest to.

But there have been some really difficult times for my family and I. In fact, far from being *grateful*, there were years in which I was frequently angry – and mostly angry at myself, by the way. I found myself suffering with decisions and choices that I had made – and risks that I took, quite frankly - that put me, and my family, in a rather precarious position.

5

There were times when I was positively miserable about leaving to go to a personal appearance, an autograph signing, whatever. I was cranky. I was irritable. I was just…not a fun person to be around. I soon realized, as did my wife, Loree, that the pattern was always the same: every time I had to go out of town, I would turn into a person, if given the opportunity, to be avoided at all costs.

And then, of course, when I came home after doing an event, my attitude would get even worse.

At one point in time, if you said I would be driving eight hours to appear on an independent wrestling show, I would think you were smoking crack.

Nuts. They're going freaking nuts. I just walked out, here in Albuquerque, in front of this crowd for the very first time. They're about to see me verbally spar - something I can do very well - but not with Vince McMahon, or Hulk Hogan, or 'Stone Cold' Steve Austin. Rather, it is *Hobo Hank* who is to be my adversary on this night. He's really getting into it, jumping into the audience and doing crazy stuff like eating people's hot dogs. Talk about living the character. Talk about living in the moment! This is what it's all about.

You know what? If I start to think about that show in Albuquerque much longer, I'll start to well up. I'll start to get tears in my eyes, purely because the energy – the sheer *energy* – is something that remains palpable to this day. I think I may have had more fun than even the talent did – just feeling that energy, and seeing the appreciation of the audience and performers alike. It elevated them, I think, in the sense that someone who didn't have to go to their show, was, in fact, there as a participant on their show. I would like to think that my presence helped bring more attention to them.

To this day, about two or three times a year, I'll get a message on social media from someone who was there that day.

Now I'm welling up again.

Shut up.

By now, you may have figured out something: this will be no ordinary pro wrestling autobiography. While granted, this is a story about what's happened in my life over the past 15 years, it's also about some of the broader lessons I learned along the way. Now don't get me wrong: throughout this book, there will be more than enough rasslin' talk to shake a stick at. TNA? It's all here. My relationship with Hulk Hogan? Read on. My return to WWE in 2019? The Hall of Fame? AEW? Yes, yes and yes.

Equally, however, I hope you take away some useful insights about some of the other topics that are important to me: life, death, family, relationships, business and perhaps some things you've rarely heard me talk about – until now.

I'm about to surprise you – *again*.

7

Mid-life Crisis 1-Me 0

2

As 2006 rolled to a close, life was pretty frickin' good. *Controversy Creates Cash* continued to make waves; my television production company, *Bischoff-Hervey Entertainment* (BHE), persisted in doing business with almost every major cable outlet, and the launch of *EricBischoff.com* provided fans with an interactive forum – given social media was still in its infancy – to respond to my often incendiary(!) commentaries on wrestling, news, politics and beyond.

I found it gratifying to connect with fans who had enjoyed (or perhaps hated) my turn as the evil General Manager of *Raw* with WWE. My on-screen exit from the program - which involved Vince McMahon tossing me into a trash compactor (*my* idea, by the way) – served as a perfect bookend, I thought, to a wrestling career that had been highly unlikely from the outset.

Although I remained under contract with WWE (my deal would eventually expire in mid-2007), my absence as a character from TV - as an on-screen performer – provided some measure of relief to an already overcrowded schedule (personal fault admission: it's in my nature to stretch myself *too thin*). All of a sudden, I was now in my early fifties, with wrestling seemingly behind me - and an unknown (yet enticing) path ahead of me.

I didn't feel like I was getting older; in fact, the thought never really dawned on me – until one fateful night in Salt Lake City.

It was just after New Year's – Friday, January 5th, 2007, to be exact. Imagine leaving home for a business meeting, and then returning to tell your wife that her 52-year-old husband broke his arm in a nightclub while he was away.

Yeah, yeah…I know. But the actual story is even more ridiculous.

I can explain – sort of. A few months prior to this, ahem, incident, BHE and Socko Energy had struck a deal to launch the *Hogan Energy* drink across the United States. As BHE had been responsible for putting the necessary license agreements together, the owners of Socko (Mike Jannicelli and Jordan Harwood) asked me to visit Salt Lake City, meet with their sales people, and discuss how best to sell the product at retail.

Following the meeting, we all went out for dinner, at which point Mike and Jordan asked if I wanted to see their newest nightclub – *The Hotel*, so named because the club was previously the site of an historic hotel building. We got there around 8:00pm, taking in this beautiful, three-stories high, woodwork-laden, wide-open space that was getting busier with patrons by the minute.

The local radio station is here, Mike then informed me.

They're doing a broadcast from our club. How about you do an interview with them, liven things up a little?

As you might imagine, I was *more* than happy to cut a couple of promos on the assembled crowd. More than simply 'liven things up,' it was probably more accurate to say that I *stirred* things up once the microphone was in my hand.

It was fun. I had a couple of cocktails when the radio DJ asked if I would do another live 'promo.'

I challenge anyone in the city of Salt Lake, I said defiantly, *to come down to The Hotel and arm wrestle me!*

The sobering reality, if you will, is that I've never actually been good at arm wrestling. Even when I was in my twenties, and working out all of the time, I wasn't any good at arm wrestling. Even in my thirties, and after having hosted some events for *Arm Wrestling International* on ESPN, I wasn't any good at arm wrestling. So "why in the hell," I later asked the readers of *EricBischoff.com*, "did I think at age 52, I should go on live radio and challenge an entire city to come down and arm wrestle?"

I initially thought it was the promoter in me, knowing my challenge would bring in a crowd. It worked, by the way – and before I knew it, I was locked up with some 20-something kid who looked like he practically *lived* in the gym. He seemed to have no idea how to arm wrestle, but he was younger and definitely in better shape than I was. Nonetheless, I whipped him pretty easily.

A few minutes later, I was locked up with another guy – late twenties, maybe early thirties. He was about my weight at the time – maybe 215, 225 – and as I recall, he had a solid, stocky frame. Anyway, I got a good jump on this sucker too, and before you know it, it looked like I was gonna go *2-0*.

I rolled my wrist over the top of his, started pulling him into my chest, and then...I heard it. It sounded like a 2x4 breaking.

It was my arm!

Initially, while I had definitely felt some kind of sharp pain, it didn't really seem that bad...until I lost all of my strength completely. I

11

stood up - trying valiantly to 'shake it off' - but my arm had other ideas.

It didn't shake at all.

It may have been wishful thinking, but at first, I wondered if maybe I had torn a muscle. It looked serious enough, however, that Mike wanted to take me to the emergency room. Once we got there, the doctor x-rayed my arm, shook his head, put me in a splint and sent me on my way.

It turned out that I had suffered a *radial fracture* in the upper part of my arm, with the break starting about an inch above my elbow (and going to about 2 ½ inches below my shoulder). The worst part was afterwards, when I had to walk around for three weeks in a compression cast, waiting to be operated on (in order to have a titanium plate screwed into my arm). After waiting for ten days to see if the bone could heal *without* surgery – as had been recommended to me – I then found out that surgery would be required after all. I *then* found out that the surgeon was on vacation, and I would have to wait another week-and-a-half to get the procedure done.

"When I got home," I lamented on *EricBischoff.com*, "and had to explain to my wife what had happened…it finally started to dawn on me. It wasn't the 'promoter in me,' or the fact that all of a sudden, I thought that I became a competitive arm wrestler.

"I just like doing some of the same stupid stuff that I've always liked doing, and by continuing to do these things, I can try and fight the fact that I'm actually getting older.

"Current score," I summarized, "Mid-life crisis 1-Me 0. But I want a rematch!"

In retrospect, it was pretty unlikely that the whole arm-wrestling escapade was going to work out for me. Then again, it was *also* unlikely that an average guy in Minneapolis, thirty-something years old – although a wrestling fan – ended up succeeding in *professional* wrestling. To be clear: I had never thought about, dreamed about, worked towards, or aspired to be involved in the actual wrestling business, but ultimately – for a period of time - I ended up as President of a division of Turner Broadcasting that produced pro wrestling at the highest level in the world.

It's all pretty unlikely, but for many reasons - some of which have been documented elsewhere – my career in wrestling almost never happened at all.

Here's one reason that I have *never* talked about.

One of the most influential people in my life was Bob Racioppi, a neighbor of mine in Pittsburgh. Bob was about 26 when we met – I was about 13 (that age difference seemed like *a lot* back then) – and he was something like a big brother to me. Bob was a very physical guy - a Vietnam veteran and a martial artist, among many other things – who ultimately started my fascination with the Old West. You can probably draw a straight line between Bob's influence on me and my eventual decision to live in Wyoming.

We met in 1968. Fast forward to 1976, and by now, I was living in Minneapolis, operating a landscape construction company and making some serious money in the process. Bob and I were still very close, and right around Thanksgiving, I went to visit him and his wife back in Pittsburgh (by this point, Bob was a very successful advertising executive for a company called Reuben H. Donnelly).

While I was there visiting, Bob couldn't stop talking about Wyoming.

Eric, let me tell you - I went to Wyoming on an elk hunt last year.

Up in the mountains. We packed up on horses, stayed in tents and man, what did we see?

Grizzly bears, elk, deer...

Prior to my family moving to Pittsburgh, I spent my childhood in Detroit – watching *Bonanza, The Virginian, Gunsmoke* and all the classic Westerns – and consequently, Bob's testimony was captivating to me.

Listen, Eric, he said. *Why don't you come out to Wyoming next summer?*

You can come out for the 4th of July and meet me out there.

At the time, I was very much into photography – a passion of mine that first began in high school. I actually created my own 'dark room' to process 35mm black-and-white film – courtesy of tearing out the bathroom in a four-wheel truck camper – which I planned to utilize once I arrived in Wyoming.

I pulled into the state at about six o'clock in the morning – and I immediately fell in love. By the time I was eating lunch, I was having the same thought over and over again: *Someday, I'm gonna live here.*

I don't know how – I don't know when – but someday, it's gonna happen.

(It took 20 years, but in 1997, my wife and I finally built our home in Wyoming.)

A lot of my fascination with Wyoming is related to its history. I was fascinated – and remain so - with Native American history. I was also fascinated with the history of the West – how it was settled and how it transformed the United States – and all the good (and bad) that came along with it.

It was a wonderful trip - but my next visit to Wyoming came under different circumstances. Bob had recently built an old farmhouse in Pennsylvania – he remodeled the whole thing himself – and was raising quarter horses on quite a bit of acreage.

As Bob had quite a bit of money at the time, he was planning to invest some funds into buying a business in Wyoming.

I was going to be involved, too – the two of us, believe it or not, were going to buy (and operate) a mountain lodge, right outside Yellowstone National Park.

I was ready to sell everything. As far as I was concerned, I was going to run this guest ranch, hunt, and spend the rest of my time taking pictures. That was my goal.

We started negotiations to purchase the business, but while we were out there, the owner of the lodge died unexpectedly. It was now left to his three children to determine the fate of the property. At first, two of the children wanted to sell the business to us, but one of them didn't. As time went on, the one who didn't want to sell suddenly wanted to – but now the other two didn't.

It went on like this until Bob and I realized that it wasn't going to get sorted out. The more time that went by, the more entrenched each of them became in whatever their latest position was. We tried to stay there as long as we possibly could, but once there was talk of lawyers getting involved, I packed up and went back to Minnesota.

Bob stayed – he always wanted to live that cowboy lifestyle - and ultimately, he went to work on a ranch called the *Two Dot Ranch*, one of the biggest ranches in the state. He was doing the same things that cowboys were doing 150 years earlier – and he was never happier.

We stayed in touch until one day in 1982. We were talking on the phone when Bob told me about an excruciating pain he was having in his right arm. He had evidently been out throwing a football, but he couldn't figure out why his arm was hurting him so much. It wasn't a muscle ache, or anything like that – it was *different*, he said.

It turns out that Bob had been exposed to Agent Orange while in the air force in Vietnam. He visited the doctor's office to find out what was causing his pain - only to be told that he had bone cancer.

He died about two months later.

I was just thinking about that this morning: *Man, how different life could have been.*

I was just a kid back then, but I've never forgotten Bob. I eventually learned the same lesson everyone does: as you get older, you lose more people that are close to you – unfortunately, in my business, that's often earlier than expected – and consequently, you start thinking about *the clock*. There *is* a clock – that's just reality – and it continues to tick for all of us. Well, at some point in time, it *stops* ticking, and that feeling gets *realer* as you get older.

Whenever my clock stops ticking, I want to do everything in my power to avoid the following scenario: being hooked up, for an extended period of time, to some kind of machine - and having friends and family feel obligated to spend time with me. I wouldn't want them to feel that way, nor would I want them to see me in that state.

I've been in that kind of position with my mother, who fought the bastard - cancer – on two different occasions. She kicked it the first time, but when it eventually got her the second time, there was a point in which she was communicating, so to speak, *with her eyes only*. I was in the position of trying to 'hear' what she was saying to me, and to this day, I can only imagine what it was.

I may have been projecting this feeling onto myself, but honestly, I don't think my mother wanted us to see her in that state. While I think she probably appreciated the fact that we loved her – and wanted to be around her – I don't think she wanted us to feel that kind of sadness. I think it hurt her to see *us* like that, if that makes any sense.

As a result of that experience, I wouldn't want my kids to go through what myself, my brother or my sister went through (especially my sister, who took it the hardest of all of us).

It was April 11th, 2007, when my Mom – Carol Ann Bischoff – died at the age of 70.

Mom was the person for whom *Controversy Creates Cash* was dedicated to. In the book, I briefly described her second battle with

17

the bastard – and how she was characteristically doing her best to fight it.

I can assure you of one thing – she kicked the bastard's ass until her very last day.

Struggling to Comprehend

3

There are times in life when one can recall exactly where they were, and exactly who they were with. There have been several such moments throughout my life, and the Chris Benoit double murder-suicide was one of them.

On Monday, June 25th, 2007, I happened to be in Pittsburgh - with Hulk Hogan - for a business meeting involving a dozen or so other people. We were joined at a restaurant by some of the top executives from GNC, the largest health food store in the country. For some time, the GNC suits had been thinking about getting involved with Hulk for a line of nutritional products and specifically, an energy drink already in national distribution with Walmart.

Just as the conversation got underway, I briefly stepped out to take a phone call, thinking nothing of it initially. It was Dallas Page on the other end of the line.

I don't remember exactly what he said, only that Page was trying his best to articulate the horrifying news - that Chris Benoit, formerly one of the best wrestlers in WCW and, at that time, a prominent star with WWE, had apparently been found dead - along with his wife, Nancy, and their seven-year old son, Daniel.

I was stunned - so much so, in fact, that I almost had no feelings about it. I guess I didn't quite know *how* to feel - it was all simply too hard to believe. My initial skepticism was fueled further by the sheer number of holes in the initial story. The information seemed a little sketchy at first - there was more that we didn't know than what we did know.

Regrettably, I've also seen people in this industry pull some pretty horrible gags, or 'ribs' as they are called in the wrestling business. I can recall a WCW event in Baltimore, for example, whereby Bret Hart received a message that his father had passed away. It wasn't true - not in the slightest - but somebody thought it would be 'funny' to play that prank on Bret. Maybe that's another reason why I was reluctant to believe the Benoit news - not only was it hard to digest, just to begin with, but part of me hoped it may have been a really sick rib or 'joke' that was getting passed around.

From across the restaurant, I looked back at our table as Page continued, noticing that Hulk was staring right back at me. Momentarily, I saw Hulk look down to read a text from his phone, and then, as he looked up, his eyes said the rest. He knew, too - and soon would the entire country.

On a personal level, I was never very close to Chris (although, in retrospect, I was as close to him as a *business* relationship would allow). I didn't socialize with Chris, neither did we spend any time after shows together. He was always quiet - kind of a loner, to be honest - and he kept to a very small group of friends. I never really saw Chris socializing after a show, at least in the same way as I did other people. So while I don't want to imply that I knew him well, I felt like I knew him well *enough* that what I was hearing from Page was simply not fathomable. I never saw any anger issues, rage issues - or anything of the sort - despite the fact that Chris performed, at a very high level, as a participant in a very physical form of entertainment, one that often depicts violence, aggressiveness, and physicality. It was pretty much consensus opinion that Chris was one of the best at it.

The way Chris carried himself outside of the ring suggested, at least to me, that he was a very soft spoken, introverted, almost gentle guy. He didn't react much to frustrations, whether they related to creative issues or otherwise – unlike a lot of his contemporaries. When I think about Eddie Guerrero, or Dean Malenko, or especially Chris Jericho - or any number of other people in WCW at the time - they often wore their emotions on their sleeves. With Eddie, for example, I always knew *exactly* what he was thinking, and consequently, there were times in which he became a little difficult to manage. There were instances where he and I would get into *heated* discussions - the most famous of all featuring my supposed decision to 'throw a cup of coffee' at him backstage (to clarify, I once threw a plastic mug of coffee on the floor - in frustration - and some coffee happened to splash on Eddie. Even to this day, if you look at my social media, there will be all kinds of memes about that incident, including a depiction of me throwing a *pot* of coffee directly at him!).

In that respect, Chris was the exact opposite of someone like Eddie. He was very business-like. He was open-minded. When he heard something that he didn't really like, or didn't feel comfortable with, he would tend to talk it through with me. He'd give his opinion, and if there was a compromise at the end of that talk - great. If there was no compromise, that would signal the end of the conversation, really. *And that was it.* So we discussed things, and at the end, Chris wouldn't display any visible emotion, at least anything that would indicate something beyond, 'Okay - we've had our discussion. I've shared my opinion with you, and this is what I believe. If you don't agree with my opinion, I'll go out and do what you want me to do.'

In that sense, some have used the term 'professional's professional' with regard to Chris and his approach to professional wrestling. In some well documented cases, after all, professional wrestling has sometimes been a very *unprofessional* environment - especially when involving creative issues with talent - but I saw no indications of that with Chris.

So I was just shocked; stunned; floored. I just didn't *see it*; I didn't see any indications of it. What I saw most in Chris, when Nancy was around or his kids were around, was almost the idyllic image of a loving husband and father. Then, after receiving the news, it was kind of a head-on collision between the reality of the situation and my pre-existing perception of Chris. I couldn't understand it; I was just numb.

It wasn't until hours later, subsequent conversations, and more information coming out - that Chris had murdered Nancy and Daniel, before hanging himself - that I became *overwhelmingly* sad. For the kids, and for Nancy...I couldn't even really imagine. I couldn't comprehend what happened to Chris that made him snap that way.

Beyond being sad, I remained thoroughly confused.

In the days and weeks thereafter, there was a significant - and at times rather disgraceful - media firestorm that followed. As more details dripped out, I was actually interested - at first - because I was still trying to understand *how* it could have happened, or *why* it could have happened. The picture slowly started becoming a little bit clearer, based on interviews with people who had recently spoken to Chris, and the corresponding timeline of events.

Ultimately, however, the coverage didn't really answer any of the important questions, as far as I was concerned. It actually created more of them – and I found myself tuning *out* of the coverage.

While as a general rule, I try not to dwell on disasters or negative things, I was wary not to allow myself to go into this 'rabbit hole,' so to speak. I decided that it wasn't going to be healthy to travel too deep into the issue; therefore, there was no contribution that I could really make - I was just on the sidelines, like everybody else, contemplating this incredibly sad event.

It was clear that this all was going to result in a big blow for the wrestling business, and so part of me was curious to see how WWE was going to react. Over the course of the prior few decades, when people in wrestling had been guilty of excessive behavior - there was a widely publicized issue with steroids, for example - such coverage had seriously hurt the business. But this was on another level, and therefore, I wondered about the impact that it could have on advertisers, and the reputation of the industry more broadly. I thought a lot about how WWE - and the wrestling industry as a whole - could be sent back to where it had been in the early '90s.

At the time, there was still a very fragile relationship between WWE, its wrestling product and potential national advertisers. But in my view, WWE ended up handling the situation as well as it possibly could have been handled. They were very strategic in what they did, and ultimately, it didn't seem to have the impact on the business that I was fearful of. I was never made aware, for example, of a lot of chatter concerning major advertisers pulling their product because of what happened.

The fallout might have been different today. If something like this happened in 2022 - God forbid - I'm not so sure WWE, or any wrestling company, would be able to get past it quite so painlessly.

On Thursday, June 28th, 2007, I summarized my feelings on the tragedy - as best as I could - in an update to *EricBischoff.com*:

I cannot begin to articulate my feelings about the tragedy in the Benoit family. It is something I am really struggling to comprehend.

I heard the news late Monday afternoon just as I was sitting down in a business meeting in Pittsburgh, I sat stunned as I listened to DDP on the other end of the phone, trying to tell me what happened. My meeting went very late into the evening and there was little new information when I went to bed.

My phone rang at 7am on Tues and the caller ID revealed a 404 area code. Assuming it was someone that I used to work with in the area, I answered the phone. It was a local sports/talk show in the Atlanta area and they wanted to get my comments. I hesitated, but since the radio personality was a friend of a friend, I decided to go ahead.

The questions started out OK...what one would normally expect in a situation like this. However they quickly turned into a "who's to blame" line of questioning and went downhill from there.

It's really impossible anymore to be honest about something as tragic and emotionally charged as this issue without sounding like I have some kind of "hidden agenda". It's clear that the media wants to blame steroids, professional wrestling, Vince McMahon, or anyone or anything else that further sensationalizes this family tragedy.

I refuse to join the choir.

I don't have enough information. I wasn't there. I am not a psychiatrist. I just can't imagine how or why this could have happened.

God bless Nancy and Daniel. God forgive Chris Benoit.

The Rear-View Mirror

4

In August 2007, my contract with WWE officially expired, and once again, I prepared to put wrestling in the *rear-view mirror* (a phrase that those close to me have heard uttered on countless occasions!). After a very successful tenure, my character as General Manager had clearly run its course, and consequently, there were no new stories to tell - or new ways of telling the same stories. When WWE called me with their decision not to renew my deal, I understood the move completely.

I couldn't complain. I had been making $350,000 a year in exchange for working, essentially, one day a week on the *Raw* schedule. I had certainly enjoyed my run, but my *heat*, or the level of vitriol that I had from the wrestling audience, was starting to subside before my final on-screen appearance. It may not have been perceptible from the outside, but I could *feel it* – and it was time to move on.

Before I became a free agent, the company asked if I would participate in an intriguing roundtable discussion – the highlights of which aired on WWE's *Classics on Demand* service – based around the subject of (what else?) the *Monday Night Wars* era. Having some non-TV business to discuss with the licensing people at WWE (BHE was preparing to launch, again in partnership with Socko, the *Raw Attitude* energy drink), I jumped at the chance to take my wife Loree to New York, the location of the shoot, for a few days around filming.

I distinctly remember two things about the discussion. Firstly, as it relates to the format, we were all (myself, Jerry Lawler, Mick Moley, Michael Hayes, and Jim Ross) encouraged to talk about the topic in a 'freeform' manner. No scripts. No censorship.

No bullshit.

That was refreshing. Secondly, although it may seem quaint now, it was the first time that the viewing audience actually got to see an authentic debate of perspectives, relative to those who were physically in the epicenter of the ratings war. Prior to this panel discussion, fans had mainly been exposed to WWE's 'version' of the war, as reflected in the 2004 video, *The Monday Night War: WWE Raw vs. WCW Nitro*, for example.

On this occasion, however, the episode turned out to be a pretty fair retrospective. It was relaxed, informal and much more honest than I had previously expected. Fans actually got to hear me say my piece – going back-and-forth with Mick Foley, most notably – in a way that hadn't been possible before.

By the time the show aired in August, I felt very comfortable with moving on from WWE – and potentially from wrestling.

In the meantime, Jason Hervey (my business partner with BHE) and I considered how we might leverage my wrestling experience to further the growth of our company. In some ways, it was an ironic discussion, given that my initial interest in producing other forms of television, after all, came out of a dissatisfaction with wrestling - when I was first employed at WCW.

It all began when Bill Watts, a well-known regional wrestling promoter, was hired by Turner Broadcasting to run WCW in 1992. At the time, despite being a third-string announcer, it was apparent to me that Watts wasn't going to change WCW - or have any positive impact at all, for that matter. I just didn't believe in anything he was attempting to do.

The morale in WCW was terrible - worse than it ever had been – and I had made up my mind to leave. It was high time, I thought back then, to take whatever experience I had gained up to that point, and explore if I could create some new opportunities outside of wrestling.

I knew I had at least a few things going for me: a little bit of creativity, about five years of experience in televised wrestling, and a keen interest in the TV business generally. I wondered if I could, once my WCW contract expired, segue into a more 'mainstream' type of television, and to that end, I started working on a television show for kids.

As I touched on in *Controversy Creates Cash*, my idea was to develop a live action show *based* on wrestling (not a wrestling show, *per se*, but thematically something similar). The concept would feature kids competing with a wrestler as their partner – and going up against other kids who were teamed up with other wrestlers. Together, they would compete in a series of fun, creative and physical (albeit non-contact!) challenges against each other. Think *American Gladiators* for kids – that's really what the show was about.

At that time, Jason, formerly a star on the ABC show *Wonder Years* - one of the highest rated shows on television – happened to be dating WCW's Missy Hyatt. As a result, Jason and I became acquainted and ultimately became good friends. We went out to Los Angeles together, pitched my idea for the kids show to a fantastic

27

woman at Fox, Molly Miles, who loved it so much that Fox made a commitment for the show (the network had a 'kids block' that ran on Saturday mornings until noon).

Eventually, time went by, and Fox didn't exercise their option for the show. It turned out that Molly left the company – she was transferred to work at the Universal Theme Park – and concurrently, Bill Watts was fired by WCW anyway. Ironically, the shelved project ended up featuring in my interview to become part of management at WCW.

When Bill Shaw – the VP of Human Resources at Turner, then-temporarily in charge of WCW because it was an HR nightmare – conducted interviews for a new Executive Producer role, he was looking for someone with a different vision.

What would you do differently? he asked.

What new ideas do you have for WCW that haven't been done yet?

In anticipation of those kinds of questions, I actually brought the presentation we had made for Fox to the Executive Producer interview. There were a number of storyboards involved, and as I recall, it made for quite the visual aid. I don't know if Bill loved the actual *idea*, by the way, but I think he appreciated my thinking outside of the typical wrestling mentality. I was looking at ways to grow the brand – to grow WCW – via targeting a completely different audience. I don't want to speak for him, but I think Bill recognized that as something unique, at least compared to what he'd been hearing in the other interviews. As has since become wrestling lore, I ended up getting the job as Executive Producer.

Eventually, as wrestling fans are familiar with, I became a Vice President, Senior Vice President and ultimately, President of WCW. In those kinds of high-profile roles, and especially given the success we were having, I was absolutely *consumed* with what I was doing. By that point, I wasn't thinking much about producing television shows for anybody else – I was just focused on wrestling.

WCW closed its doors in March 2001 - a saga that won't be revisited for the purposes of this book. At that stage, I was still relatively young, suddenly more interested in producing mainstream television – or something other than wrestling, at least - and I had quite a few contacts in Hollywood. I had an agent at CAA. I had decent relationships with various network executives. Just from my time at WCW, I'd taken meetings with Peter Liguori, who was the head of FX at the time, and Kevin Reilly, who ultimately went to Turner – and was the person responsible for bringing AEW into Turner many years later.

Meanwhile, Jason and I continued our friendship, and I became very close with his family, too. He had transitioned to becoming an executive at HealthSouth, a massive healthcare company that hired him as a Senior VP of media and communications. Well…things kind of 'went south' at HealthSouth. The CEO of the company was indicted in a number of SEC violations, and the FBI conducted a night raid of the company's headquarters (the corporation would be charged with overstating its profits to the tune of $1.4 billion).

It all went down right before *Wrestlemania* in Seattle, around March of 2003. I was actually preparing to go to the event when Jason called me – essentially with a message of concern for his future. He had moved his family to Alabama, after all, which is where HealthSouth was located, and he was pretty distraught because of everything that was going on. I told him, 'Jason, just jump on a plane and meet me in Seattle. Let's hang out at *Wrestlemania* and figure things out.'

29

Jason had been in the television and movie industry since he was five years old. The business was in his family – Jason's uncle, for example, remains a financial advisor to some of the biggest names in Hollywood (having managed investments for Roy Disney, Clint Eastwood and Barbara Streisand, among others). With this in mind, Jason and I knew that we had access to various high-profile talent, whether it be through our agents (we were both represented by CAA at the time), or simply through our own individual 'rolodexes' of contacts. We decided to take a swing at making the most of these contacts, and soon after, Bischoff-Hervey Entertainment – our own independent television production company – was born.

At that time, so-called 'reality' television was really starting to emerge. It had been around for a while – MTV, famously, started it all with *Real World* – and there were some foreign formats, particularly from the UK, that were having success in the United States. *Survivor* was probably the first *really* big hit that completely changed the landscape, and 'reality' (i.e. 'non-scripted') TV took off thereafter.

Jason and I thought that through taking advantage of our resources, connections and experience, we could start creating our *own* reality television shows. As a result of Jason growing up in Hollywood – and being a pretty big star there – he had a lot of contacts who, quite frankly, were always looking for something to do. It soon became easy for us to start pitching shows - and to put deals together.

The first show that we produced was called *I Want To Be A Hilton* for NBC, in association with a Dutch company called Endemol. Not so coincidentally, it happened to be Jason's relationship with the Hilton family that made it possible for us to attach them to the project. We made good money on the show, and more importantly, it increased our profile, which is a vital part of launching your own production company. The fact that we now had a hit on NBC – with a name like the Hilton family, no less – allowed us to have serious conversations with a different kind of clientele.

It soon began to snowball. Celebrities started coming to *us*; ideas started coming to us. Our agents would bring us projects that they thought would be appropriate for BHE to produce. We just started cranking out television projects – eventually producing them for VH1, MTV, TruTV, A&E and AMC, among many others. By 2007, we were well on our way to having an enormous amount of success.

In retrospect, I can see that one of the advantages we had – as freshly minted independent television producers, with no previous experience in the non-scripted format – was experience in directing so-called 'non-professional' talent. From about 1996 or so, after I got into management at WCW, Jason and I worked together on some WCW-themed projects (the WCW home video series, for example). Clearly, I already had the experience in dealing with 'non-professional' talent (i.e. talent without formal training as actors), but through these projects, Jason learned a lot about dealing with them, too.

Personally, if I would have tried to produce a *scripted* program - or tried to direct a scripted television show - I would have been horrible at it. Producing and directing professional actors and actresses requires a completely different skill set than producing and directing non-professional talent. Interestingly, we noticed over time that some of the actors and actresses who were really good in *formal* acting roles, kind of sucked at being themselves. They had a hard time making themselves interesting in a *non-scripted* way.

In addition to this awareness, vis-à-vis the distinction between professional and non-professional talent, I also already knew how to 'hook' an audience (although in fairness, I know *much* more about it now!). I knew how to keep their interest for a given period of time - and how to 'pay off' a show in a manner where viewers would want to check out the next episode.

My experience with *Nitro* taught me how to utilize *cliffhangers*, and essentially, how to become appointment television. I wanted people to feel like they couldn't miss next week's episode; that they couldn't *afford* to turn the channel. It ended up having a direct application to the shows that I would later be involved in.

Jason and I just complimented each other so well. As Jason was an actor, he often brought a different perspective to the table than I did, and therefore, he was able to contribute ideas in a very unique way. Whereas my approach was mainly based on my experience in the wrestling business – in addition to pure instinct (I've always been good at reading people and evaluating their strengths) – his approach was rooted in the experience of being around a variety of big-budget movies and television shows (along with the producers and directors who worked on them). Over time, BHE became known for getting the most out of people, and networks trusted our ability to find and retain an audience.

After several years in operation, Jason and I developed a great relationship with Melanie Moreau, a very creative and fun executive at CMT (Country Music Television). Melanie had an ability to know exactly what her audience was looking for, and although CMT was still very much a country music kind of platform, they were starting to move away from that brand identity.

In television at the time, the trend *du jour* was seeing celebrities participate in competitive events, packaged in an elimination format. The trend seemed to be reaching a peak right about the time that Melanie, Jason and I went to dinner one night. As an executive,

Melanie was in a position where she was hearing 'pitches' all day long, which provided us with a lot of insight as to where things were going in the business. We talked about how Jason and I could package some of the celebrity relationships that we had into something that her network was looking for.

That led us to kicking around doing something with wrestling, although at first, I wasn't necessarily excited about *celebrities* learning how to wrestle (the concept that eventually formed the basis of *Hulk Hogan's Celebrity Championship Wrestling*). I kind of thought, 'Celebrities learning to wrestle? This is gonna look sloppy. It's going to disappoint the wrestling fans out there, and it's not going to be compelling for the non-wrestling fans.'

It didn't strike me as a home run, but if we were going to do it, I thought, we needed to use 'real' people - or 'regular' people, for lack of a better word - who actually wanted to learn. They could learn how to wrestle under the tutelage of Hulk Hogan – that was my original take on the idea. We could bring people in, put them through a real training situation, and expose them to the same kind of grueling challenges and character-building exercises that you would see in a professional wrestling training center (think of an abridged version of WCW's Power Plant, if you will).

That concept is what I was passionate about, and Melanie loved it, too. She saw a lot of value in Hulk, and she knew that it would be a big hit for her audience - her demo. When we eventually pitched it up to CMT, they said, 'We love it, too…but we actually want to capitalize on the celebrity competition elimination format. We want to do this with celebrities.'

I was really hesitant, just from a practical perspective, in terms of what this would look like on television. On the other hand, it was the job of Jason and I to deliver what CMT wanted. We soon got to the business of finding the right celebrities for the concept.

33

Admittedly, we ended up featuring mostly 'B level' celebrities – people that weren't out making movies for millions of dollars, for sure – but public figures who were certainly well known, and definitely still active in the entertainment business. As long as they had some equity within the general mainstream audience, that's what CMT were looking for.

The first thing that I did was get a hold of Dennis Rodman. I had worked with Dennis quite a bit – we were friends by this point – and he jumped right in with both feet.

When I brought Dennis to WCW in 1997, he and Hulk clicked immediately - it was just uncanny how they clicked, and the respect they had for each other. There was something about their respective personalities - just chemistry, I guess – that caused them to bond immediately. Even to this day, I think Dennis *loves* Hulk - and the opposite is true, also.

That dynamic may exist because they've both kind of gone through similar things, and consequently, they probably understand each other in ways that the rest of us can't relate to. On an intellectual level, you could *try* and understand what their lives are like, or maybe read a book or listen to some stories about it. However, until you've lived that kind of existence (particularly with respect to the pressure cooker that is the media), you really have no clue what it's like.

Years later, when all the negative headlines came out with regard to Hulk's lawsuit with Gawker, Dennis was one of the first people to reach out to Hulk in support. Dennis is a unique cat – everyone knows that – but he's actually one of the more intelligent people that I've ever sat down and had a conversation with. People may look at him based on what they see in the media, or what the various headlines might be, but they don't know the real person – like I do.

34

In terms of life experience and understanding people – the actual *nature* of people - Dennis is actually a very enlightened guy. I've had deep conversations with Dennis that you would never have thought possible.

In addition to Rodman, Jason reached out to a number of other people for the show, including Danny Bonaduce, who was one of the most successful DJs in the country at the time. Danny had a massive footprint in the radio business, and we knew we would get a lot of promotion, hype and awareness as a result. Jason also got us Erin Murphy, who played Tabitha on *Bewitched* – someone who I would never have thought of. Dustin Diamond of *Saved By The Bell* fame was another participant, as was Frank Stallone, and Todd Bridges from *Different Strokes*. We had an amazing level of interest from all of those people.

I think our contestants viewed the show as a genuine opportunity – to get some face time, increase their equity with the audience, and in some cases, even jump start their careers. We got CMT to write a hefty check for the series, and once we communicated who was on board, we knew the network's excitement was such that they would promote the hell out of it (as I recall, CMT committed to a budget of $750,000 per episode, of which BHE received a margin of 35% - 10% for our role as executive producers, and 25% in consideration of production fees, as in this case, we produced the show ourselves). Once it came time to negotiate contracts with the talent, however, things got a little *interesting* (let's just say that celebrities often have varying opinions of their value).

We went and found an old warehouse in Southeast LA – kind of a run down, beat up, imposing facility that had the look we were hoping for. We didn't want the show to be glitzy – we wanted it to look kind of *gritty* - and consequently, the environment had a kind of personality to it. It wasn't always easy to film the show – there wasn't air conditioning (and it was August!) - but everyone was so excited that they worked their asses off anyway.

It all really surprised me. I didn't think the contestants would take it seriously enough, at least enough to create the kind of drama or intensity of conflict that makes a good competition reality series work. But the cast brought the intensity - in particular, Erin Murphy, who was the most surprising of them all. Erin was pretty, married, a mother with kids, and she didn't really need to go as hard as she did. She was very successful outside the entertainment industry, but for our show, she really, really *brought it*. Similarly, Dustin Diamond was someone who I thought would be more of a comedy relief challenger, but he stepped up in a serious way, too.

It ended up being a really great experience, not so much because it was a great television show or anything, but rather, because of the talent themselves. They truly put a ton of effort into what they did.

Each week after filming the show, Hulk would jump in a plane and fly back to Tampa for the weekend, typically getting back in time for the following Monday. His injuries were already starting to affect his ability to get through the 12- or 14-hour days required for filming; and concurrently, by virtue of going through a divorce from his wife Linda, he was under a massive mental strain.

For Hulk, or more accurately, Terry Bollea – the man behind the character - things were about to get worse.

Finding Hulk Hogan

5

On the night of August 26ᵗʰ 2007, Terry's son, Nick, lost control of a vehicle in Clearwater, Florida, and tragically, a passenger was left with horrible injuries requiring 24-hour-a-day care. Although he wasn't sentenced to be in isolation, Nick was basically put in solitary confinement, by virtue of the county's decision to separate the 'son of a celebrity' from the general population. He was ultimately charged with several violations for the crash - including a felony - and as his father, Terry was overwhelmingly distraught at the whole incident.

Physically, Terry was falling apart, too. His back was so bad that there were multiple times in which I went to his hotel, looking to pick him up for the show, and he couldn't get out of bed. He would have tears in his eyes when I looked at him. He was just in so much pain.

Unfortunately for Terry, the only way to deal with the pain was to use the pain meds that he had been prescribed. He needed them – he could barely walk on some days – although if you go back and watch *Hulk Hogan's Celebrity Championship Wrestling*, you would never see any indication of it.

As soon as that camera went off, though, he would emotionally and physically *collapse* – I saw it.

I was concerned for him, certainly because of the pain he was in, but also because – in addition to the things that had been prescribed to him – Terry was starting to self-medicate, too. You'd watch him take a pill of Vicodin, and then he'd follow it up with a half-bottle of Tito's vodka. It just wasn't a good situation, and as it was tough on Terry, it was tough on me, too.

One night, early in 1994, it was about one o'clock in the morning when I got a phone call at my house in Atlanta. Loree and I were in bed and had been asleep for a while, so initially I thought, 'Oh my gosh, this must be an emergency. Who calls at one o'clock in the morning?'

I got up, kind of groggy, wondering who this could possibly be.

On the other end of the line, I heard, 'Hey, brother.'

The voice, perhaps as identifiable as the Hulk Hogan look itself, was kind of a giveaway from the start. Needless to say, I woke up in a hurry, and we had a great conversation on the phone that night, relative to Terry's potential interest in joining WCW (he would eventually debut on WCW television that June).

As WCW was shooting its shows at the Disney-MGM studios, we agreed to meet up in Orlando, going to dinner a couple of times to get a feel for each other. I think Terry was kind of doing a chemistry check on me, and the opposite was true on my part, too. More than anything, however, I remember how Terry was just very down to earth. If you can imagine the scene - Hulk Hogan, sitting in a restaurant on a Disney property at eight o'clock at night - trying to discuss business with him was a real challenge. Every few seconds you would hear the famous, 'Hey Hulk, I don't mean to interrupt...', but then each and every time, someone would proceed to interrupt him - in the middle of our conversation!

38

Nonetheless, what impressed me most about Terry, in that situation, was that he remained genuinely very kind to people - and not a Hollywood kind of genuine, by the way. On the contrary, he was *truly* kind to everybody who asked for an autograph, young or old - it really didn't matter to him. He made every one of the fans feel like he was having a personal conversation with them, and that's different from a whole lot of other celebrities. I've seen others in his position say to the manager of a restaurant, 'Please keep people away from me.'

I've been around celebrities for a long time. A lot of times, there tends to be a *superficial* friendliness there; you know, 'I'm a celebrity so I can't really be mean to people. Yes, I'm gonna smile, sign the autograph and take the picture…but I wanna move on out of here pretty soon.'

In that respect, Terry was different from everybody else. Everybody that comes into contact with 'The Hulkster' feels like they know him afterwards, and consequently, there exists a connection between him and the audience that goes well beyond the wrestling persona.

I took notice of the way he treated people, and the way those conversations with fans would progress. *That* made me want to be in business with Hulk Hogan (the opportunity to sign the biggest star in wrestling didn't hurt, either).

The rest, as they say, is history, and I have recently made the argument that the acquisition of Hulk - with his name value, marketability and star power alone - was so valuable as to have practically saved WCW.

Wrestling fan or not, *everyone* knows who Hulk Hogan is. Although he would come to national prominence with the WWF in the mid-1980's, many of us still remember his debut in the AWA years earlier. As viewers, we had been hearing about this apparent monster that was coming into the territory, and one Saturday night, I remember Hulk walking into the frame with his back to the camera. In a really well-done spot, especially from a production standpoint, he did this huge bicep pose that completely ate up the television screen. It was a really memorable moment, so much so that I can remember the color of the couch I was sitting on at the time.

By the time Hulk was really taking off with the WWF, wrestling had become a national phenomenon. For those of us used to watching regional promotions with shows produced in small television studios – maybe 50 to 100 people at ringside – it was incredible to see WWF events with 40, 50 or 60 thousand people in attendance. I remember watching one day and saying to Loree, 'You know what? I've gotta find a way to meet Hulk Hogan.'

She replied, quite naturally, 'Why?'

I think she thought I was fan-boying out or something.

'Because I have an idea,' I replied, looking back at our little black-and-white TV set.

'Hulk Hoagies.'

'I mean, look at how many people are in that arena,' I continued. 'Can you imagine if they had 'Hulk Hoagies' at the concession stand?' (Being a product of the East Coast, at least for much of my life, 'subs' were always 'hoagies' to me.)

I never did get the chance to pitch the idea to Terry, but we laughed about that recently.

Initially, Terry wasn't so excited about working with me in WCW. He had just left the WWF – and all of the fallout that surrounded his departure – and I had only recently been promoted into management. He was actually far more excited about working for Turner Broadcasting, WCW's parent company, particularly because he was interested in furthering his movie and television career. Ultimately, however, what started out as a cordial relationship between us grew to the point where we became best friends.

It was in 1996, when Hulk famously turned heel and helped form the nWo, that our relationship really started to grow. He really started to trust me at that point (it's *all* about trust with Terry), and in turn, I enjoyed seeing him renew his enthusiasm for the business. I know that some fans think of the heel turn as an 'egomaniac' acting purely in his own self-interest. You know, 'Hulk Hogan just wanted to make money and he saw a big opportunity for himself.'

That's bullshit. Let me be plain: Terry Bollea didn't need the money at all. He had tens and tens (and tens) of millions of dollars in the bank, and if he decided to never work again at that point, his children, their children (and their children) would never have to work again. He wasn't doing it 'for the money', he was doing it because he loved the business, and for the first time in a long time, he saw something that actually got him excited.

As time went on, he became far more confident as a heel than he had been as a babyface during the previous two years, partly because he knew that his prior character wasn't working. About that time is when the nature of our conversations became much more personal. We talked a lot more about life, our kids, our families, and things outside of the wrestling business itself. By 1998 or so, the level of trust between us was such that our bond was pretty much solidified.

Terry was always surrounded by people that were very supportive of him, people that were 'back slappers', people that would tell him all the things that he wanted to hear. They would really play it up and act like the life of the party around him, mainly because they were looking to get something from him. I didn't approach our relationship in the same way - and I think he recognized that eventually.

That said, I think Terry *really* recognized that fact once I was no longer in a position to get anything from him. After WCW was sold, and then we both worked together again at the WWF, his divorce from Linda began a very devastating period in his life. Add to the mix his physical challenges – and the emotional fallout from Nick's terrible car accident – and we started spending a lot of time on the phone.

Things had got to the point, as he has talked about in his own book and public statements, that Terry found himself alone at home, pointing a gun to his head. He was crying out for help due to the pain that he was experiencing at that time. It got so bad that I said to Loree, 'I'm gonna go down to stay in Florida with him.'

When she asked me how long I planned to stay, I said, 'Until I'm sure he's ok.'

Prior to that decision, a couple of things had come up where Terry had called me on the phone. I would ask him what was going on, and I could tell over the phone that he was pilled up (again, I want to emphasize, this wasn't recreational stuff that he was doing. He was being prescribed some of the most powerful stuff going). While I can understand a doctor - particularly before people understood how devastating Oxycontin or Vicodin could be - looking at Hulk Hogan, a 300-pound guy, and prescribing those things to him for the pain, it had the effect of *changing* Terry.

He was becoming a different person, and I was starting to get afraid for him – afraid of his potential choices and decisions. As he had moved out of his house, he was living in a condo on the beach in Clearwater, and he was lonely. He was isolating himself more and more, which isn't terribly uncommon among people who go through the kind of issues he was facing.

I've seen it before – people get deeper and deeper into depression, and one of the first things that happens is a withdrawal from being around other people. They want to wallow in their own misery, but ideally away from others – and that was what was happening with Terry. Based on the tone of our conversations - and the subjects of those conversations – I could tell that he needed somebody to be with him.

Loree was very supportive of me going to Florida. We were lucky in that we had the financial means to allow for it, but equally, she was concerned about my friend, too.

Aside from returning home every other weekend or so, I basically lived with Terry, in that condo on the beach, for a period of about two or three months. I now had a front row seat to witness what he was going through, and it was tough. The pain was getting worse by the day, and by the time he started having trouble walking, I really started feeling horrible for him.

After all, here was this guy – *Hulk* Hogan, remember – who had basically been the epitome of strength and power for so long. Now I'd be walking next to him and thinking, 'This guy's gonna be in a wheelchair in six months.' It was that bad.

In the beginning, things were just out of control, at least in the sense that Terry didn't know which way to turn, or even what to do. He couldn't *make* anything go away simply because he was Hulk Hogan, or because he had the money to do so – none of those things mattered.

Nevertheless, he would get up early every single morning, usually around 5am. He was trying to find something to hold on to - something that would change the sorry state that he was in – and during those mornings, that meant being head down in his Bible. He'd spend at least an hour reading the Bible, coffee on, but once he was done, it was almost time to start on the phone with the attorneys

43

(sometimes for up to eight hours a day, in light of the very serious issue that Nick was involved in).

Terry was doing everything he could to help with that issue - while simultaneously dealing with his half-crazy ex-wife – *while* continuing to struggle with his physical pain (and the obvious effects of the medication that came with it). That said, I was most concerned for him when there was *nothing* going on – especially on the weekends, for example, when he didn't have the constant contact with the attorneys (as strange as that may sound).

When Terry had a lot of time on his hands, that's when I would get most concerned, and so I just stayed with him – 24 hours a day (I tried to pick my spots when going home, usually when I knew he had something going on). Sometimes, because I still had business to attend to, we wouldn't necessarily be talking all the time, but I could switch gears in two minutes if he needed me.

Even though he was struggling so much, Terry still felt the need to go to the gym, as so much of his makeup – and his persona, quite frankly – was wrapped up in his physical appearance. Occasionally, there would be a lighter moment or two (usually involving some old stories over sushi), but overall, it was just a *horrible* period of time.

He was still doing things that I wished he wouldn't do. He was still self-medicating and drinking too much, but I no longer believed there would be a horrible result. I no longer believed he would again put a gun to his head.

As time went on, with regard to Nick's situation in particular, there seemed to be light at the end of the tunnel. I knew that as long as there was hope that Nick's circumstances would change, Terry would focus on that - and ultimately, he would be fine. That's when I started feeling better about going home for a couple of days.

By the time I left for good, I was pretty comfortable in doing so.

With all due respect to my biological brother, there's no friend or sibling who I have been closer to than Terry. Our relationship is based on honesty – he's *very* honest with me, and I'm *very* honest with him. There's no agenda between us, no hidden motive or opportunity that he's trying to set me up for, or vice versa. We just have honest discussions based on two values: trust and loyalty.

To me, those values are the most important aspects of any relationship: husband-wife, employer-employee, friend-to-friend, you name it. You have to trust that someone who you're being honest with won't hold that honesty against you – hopefully because, in the sense that they value the relationship as much as you do, they exhibit loyalty in the process.

That's probably why I feel as strongly as I do about Terry. I look at all of the things that he's gone through – and all of the self-inflicted damage he's had to endure – and I can confidently say that I know the real guy. Throughout the entire Gawker incident that went down years later, while I can understand what people were thinking – based on the headlines alone – I knew how Terry *really* treated people. He never treated anybody differently, and in fact, I know that he wanted people to always feel good around him.

His state of mind was in a horrible place at that time. His self-esteem was in a horrible place at that time. He was afraid. He was mortified. He was losing his wife. He was losing his home. He was losing his career – losing his identity, really. He was losing everything that was important to him, losing everything that he loved – and it was all happening at the same time! So now throw drugs and alcohol on top of that, and you understand that people do and say stupid shit. It's not because it's really who they are – it's because of *where* they are. With this in mind, none of the horrible things that were said about Terry mattered to me – I knew the real cat.

45

With respect to Terry's perception among wrestling fans, there has been a lot written about his character – usually some variation of, 'Hulk Hogan only cares about Hulk Hogan.' It simply isn't true, although Terry *is* – without a shadow of a doubt - a very, very good businessman.

He was careful with respect to protecting his character in the wrestling business, operating in a world – let's not forget – where no-one else is going to protect your character for you. Everybody else, in fact, is more than likely going to suck the value *out* of your character, trying to take that value with them.

But countless times – outside of the ring - I've watched Terry make people from all walks of life feel special, even when he was at a low point himself. If you ran into Terry back then at some taco joint somewhere in Tampa, he would have tried his best to make your day – even if his world was falling apart around him. You don't get to meet a lot of people like that in your life.

But similar to other wealthy celebrities, Terry had people who took advantage of him, including, but not limited to, his ex-wife's family members. He bought cars, motorcycles and *homes* for family members, gave money to family members, even helped start businesses for family members. People knew that if you called him and said, 'Wanna grab a beer?', that beer would soon turn into a $600 sushi dinner.

Guess who was paying the tab?

You're like a giant apple tree, I would often tell him, *and the people you surround yourself with are busy shaking that tree, hoping that an apple will fall their way.*

To be clear, Terry didn't mind all of that. He was generous, not only from a financial point of view, but also with his time, too. He was trying to make everybody happy, and honestly, that was more important to him than the fact that people were exploiting him. He knew he was being taken advantage of - he just tolerated it, went with it. He's much better at recognizing these things now.

Once things stabilized a little bit, Terry and I took a trip - partially on business – to the *Palms Casino* resort in Las Vegas. By this point, he was heavily invested in the spiritual side of his life, talking constantly about his relationship with God, as well as his hopes that the worst of times were over. We were talking about it all one day while walking the casino floor, eventually stopping at the *Hart and Huntington* tattoo parlor (the first tattoo parlor ever located in a Vegas casino, incidentally, as depicted in the reality show *Inked*).

Terry looked at me and stopped.

I want to get the word 'grateful' tattooed on my wrist, he said.

I want to remind myself, he continued, *to be grateful for what I'm going through.*

I gotta remind myself to be grateful for today – to be grateful for having the opportunity to improve my situation.

It was really quite important to him, and the more he talked about it, the more I realized something: perhaps *I* needed to think more in those terms, too.

I was just fast forwarding through life, taking on projects, taking on opportunities, chasing the money…but I wasn't paying any attention to the things *I* had to be grateful for.

Even though I wasn't going through the same kind of despair as Terry was, I was ignoring all of the important things that were unfolding around me. I could feel it at that moment.

Later that night – our business meeting complete, and a couple of beers later – we headed right back to the tattoo place. It made for quite the story once I got home!

As I look at it now, the word *grateful* is written on the inside of *my* left wrist.

It would serve as a poignant reminder in the years to come.

History Repeated?

6

Throughout 2008 and 2009, the dirtsheets frequently exploded with speculation surrounding my future in wrestling, often linking my name (and that of Hulk's) with talks of a "new" wrestling promotion to challenge WWE. On a fairly regular basis, headlines promising an "imminent" announcement seemed to be commonplace on the various news and rumor sites. In promoting *Hulk Hogan's Championship Wrestling*, our reality show on CMT, I couldn't help but stir the pot a little, adding fuel to the fire with some comments on my own website.

"People continue to ask me," I wrote, "if I will ever get back into the wrestling business in a competitive way. I ended *Controversy Creates Cash* with six words: 'Probably not, but never say never.'

"I'm glad I did."

In the time since WCW was sold to WWE, the unfortunately-named *TNA Wrestling* (as in Total Non-Stop Action) was founded in 2002, operating exclusively as a pay-per-view operation in its infancy. In 2004, the company struck a deal with Fox Sports Net, and in 2005, it secured a Saturday night time slot with Spike TV (now known as the Paramount Network). Despite the presence of numerous former WCW (and WWE) stars on its roster, and the fact that many of the production staff in TNA had worked for me in WCW, the notion that somehow TNA was a 'spiritual successor' to WCW struck me, quite frankly, as ridiculous.

To be honest, I was never interested, at any level or at any time, in potentially working for TNA. First and foremost, I *hated* the TNA name ('T and A' – do you get it? It's just so clever.). When I heard about it for the first time, I thought, 'This just reeks of Vince Russo.'

As of mid-2009, Russo was apparently the Head of Creative at TNA, having previously failed in a similar role at WCW. His approach to creative, which happened to be incredibly juvenile, was reflected, I thought, in the name of his current employer (did I mention that I hated the fucking name, 'TNA?'). To me, it reflected a lack of everything that the wrestling business needs to be successful. It might be fitting for a fraternity, maybe – you could say, once a week or something, 'Let's have a TNA wrestling match in the frat house with a bunch of sorority girls. Let's smoke and drink and all have sex when it's over.'

That would at least make sense, but to have a nationally televised show on Spike called 'TNA'…that was embarrassing to me. Even though I had no involvement with the company, I was embarrassed for the people who did. Moreover, my feeling at that time was really, 'Been there, done that.' I thought, 'What could TNA provide me that I don't already have?' I didn't need the money, and I was making far more, at that particular time, with BHE (close to a million dollars a year) than I ever had in professional wrestling. There was no motivation – financial, personal or otherwise – to even entertain a role with TN-fucking-A.

Jason and I were having so much success, with BHE, that I doubted I would even have *time* to get involved in wrestling again. I was basically thinking, 'Okay - I went through the WCW journey, and it didn't end up the way I wanted it to end up, but the WWE opportunity came along, and it was a way for me to kind of write the end of my own story in the wrestling business.'

I had a blast working with WWE, and the more time passed since

50

my last on-screen appearance, the more I realized that it was how I wanted my public career in the wrestling business to end. From everything I had heard, anyway, TNA wasn't interested in bringing me in.

I attribute that partly to the fact that Dixie Carter, the President of TNA, wanted so badly to be recognized as the 'female Vince McMahon' that she didn't want Eric Bischoff as part of her company. Perceptually, if I was to be a part of TNA, Dixie would no longer be seen as the one 'calling the shots', and I think that was a little bit of a problem for her.

In reality, Dixie's parents - Bob and Janice Carter - were *really* the shot-callers in the TNA situation (the Carter family, owners of Panda Energy International, reportedly invested $250,000 to purchase a 71% stake in TNA, after the company nearly went out of business within a few months). I can't speak for how Bob and Janice felt about my potential involvement with TNA, but I do know one thing: they were interested in Hulk Hogan - that's for sure.

TNA had made overtures towards Hulk as early as 2003, once in an effort to promote a pay-per-view match between him and Jeff Jarrett. While previously, I wasn't involved in those conversations – I was still working for WWE – it wasn't until 2009 when TNA reached out to Hulk again. As I was still handling a lot of Hulk's business, he asked if I would be interested in making the move with him (I jokingly refer to my role in that situation as Eric Bischoff being 'Jimmy Harted' into TNA, as in years past, Hulk would rarely make any move in wrestling without bringing Jimmy along with him).

Look, if this is real, Hulk told me, *and if I end up going there...I'm only going if you go with me.*

Still in the process of moving on, relative to the various crises that had engulfed his life over the preceding few years, Hulk wasn't in a position to conduct business as usual. As a result, he 'tagged me in' to negotiate with TNA on his behalf, trusting that my intentions would always be reflected in his best interests. This followed an earlier period where I had handled, for a short time, *all* of Hulk's business interests.

There had been a point in time – at the peak of the divorce fallout, really – when Hulk actually transferred all of his assets into my name (including all of his money, quite frankly). The same was true with respect to all of his trademarks, of which fairly regular management is particularly important (if a public figure fails to keep their trademarks current, or alternatively, fails to challenge infringements on a trademark, it can be considered abandoned).

It was always intended as a short-term, temporary situation – and it was – but you should have seen my bank balance. I could have bought an island off the coast of Aruba!

Hulk knew that I wasn't interested in 'booking' TNA or anything like that. Nonetheless, he asked if I would come in and *oversee* his creative – anything that had to do with the Hulk Hogan character. We also talked about my supervision of other matters that related to his involvement with TNA - merchandising and licensing, among other areas. After all, Hulk's real value - as I had experienced first-hand in WCW – came in the opportunities that arose through Hulk Hogan being attached to the TNA property.

With Hulk Hogan on the roster, everything could potentially be made easier, whether that meant negotiating with a television partner, trying to enhance your position with a pay-per-view provider, or finding leverage in a potential licensing deal. It wasn't like Hulk was going to come in, become the TNA World

52

Heavyweight champion, and subsequently have a title reign for two or three years. His *brand equity* was the reason why, at 56, his presence came with a commensurate price tag.

Nonetheless, when it came to the creative side of TNA, Vince Russo's involvement was a major issue for both of us. While Hulk didn't necessarily hold a grudge from *Bash at the Beach 2000* - when Russo famously 'went into business for himself' (diverting from the creative that we had all, including Brad Siegel, then-President of TNT and TBS, agreed to) - there had been serious ramifications arising from that incident (including Hulk suing WCW as a result).

Hulk never had any confidence in Russo's creative abilities, but when he lost trust in Russo's integrity, too – well, that was kind of a problem. Nearly ten years later, he felt even stronger about the subject, and like myself, Hulk was wary of making the same mistake twice. *I don't know what your goals are, Eric,* he emphasized, *but I'm not going to TNA without you.*

With respect to his potential TNA move, Hulk wasn't concerned with the reaction from WWE - or Vince McMahon in particular. I don't think he viewed going to TNA as closing the door on future business dealings with Vince, with whom he enjoys a classic love-hate relationship. Long ago, I realized that the dynamic between Hulk and Vince is kind of dysfunctional in nature - it's almost like a husband and wife who are madly in love with each other one minute, but the next minute are fighting like cats and dogs. In any event, I don't think we even talked about what the reaction from the 'other side' might be - it was a total non-factor.

More important as a factor was Hulk's strong desire to remain involved in the wrestling business. Irrespective of the many challenges that he was dealing with at the time, he had spent the majority of his adult life in the industry, and like a lot of performers

- Ric Flair, Randy Savage and Roddy Piper come to mind - he had almost *become* his character. At the very least, Hulk's character had become an overwhelming part of his personal identity, and admittedly, he wasn't ready to leave that behind.

Even though it was unlikely that Hulk would perform in the ring very often, TNA were interested enough to offer him a great deal of money to sign – an amount well into the seven figures. As the company was taping all their shows in Orlando, there would be no need to travel to the events via airplane - a big issue because of Hulk's back issues and the resultant pain he was in. In that sense, in comparison to other such offers in the past, this was a much easier opportunity for Hulk.

All of the above – notably, TNA's lucrative money offer, and the convenience of Hulk only being an hour-and-a-half away from Orlando, in Tampa - added up to a very attractive deal. Before long, and in order to position myself in the role of overseeing Hulk's creative, I ended up negotiating my *own* deal with TNA. As part of the deal, I included Jason Hervey to come and work with me.

Jason and I had always split everything down the middle – 50/50 – regardless of who initiated a particular project. In my mind, this particular opportunity was no different, and so during the negotiation period, I made it clear to TNA that a) they would not be hiring Eric Bischoff, *per se*, due to the fact that b) they would be hiring Bischoff-Hervey Entertainment instead.

Jason still loved the wrestling business, and if I had entered into an agreement without him, he probably would have been very disappointed by that (and not just from a financial point of view). We shortly got the all clear that he would be coming in, too, and as such, our attorney took it from there. One of the major deal points included a suggestion that we sign a two-year deal.

Despite what may have been said elsewhere, my role in going into TNA had nothing to do with how they might brand their company, or any strategy or tactics as it relates to brand building. My role was simply to make sure that Vince Russo did not manipulate creative in a way that was going to disparage Hulk Hogan. While one could argue - and I gave an opinion along these lines to Hulk - that Hulk Hogan being involved in a wrestling company called 'TNA' was potentially damaging *enough* to his brand, it wasn't enough of a concern for it to be raised during negotiations.

At that point, there would be no discussion of changing the company name.

I *still* hated it.

For all of her faults - we all have them, as I certainly do – I very much liked Dixie Carter. She was a good person with a very good heart, and I would go as far as to say that her intentions were admirable. At first, I gave her the benefit of the doubt, trying not to be influenced by whatever her perception was at the time. Soon enough, however, it became clear to me that she didn't know anything – anything at all – about the professional wrestling business.

Dixie is a very elegant woman, and she is a very smart, classy woman. In the beginning, as I would listen to some of the people around her express their opinions, attempting to guide her or help in some way, I found myself listening to some of the most ridiculous nonsense I had ever heard. In kind of an exercise to gauge her instinct for the business, I would watch Dixie to see how she would react in those situations.

Knowledge and experience are great qualities, of course, but in my opinion, *instinct* is equally as valuable – and often more elusive. There are a lot of experienced people in the wrestling business who you might assume, based on their being in the ring for 20 or 30 years, automatically have a great instinct for it. That isn't always necessarily the case.

Based on my observations, Dixie received some suggestions that I thought were misguided, but in other cases, she was listening to shit that was frankly absurd. However, I noticed that Dixie never took a strong position on anything that was discussed or brought to her attention. She never wanted to hurt anyone's feelings, and while she made it a point to listen to everyone in the room, she really struggled with making an actual decision. When you combine that lack of instinct with zero knowledge and zero experience, she was too busy being pulled in all directions.

Contrary to what some may believe, I actually had a lot of empathy for Dixie, mainly because I remembered how much of a challenge it was to 'learn on the job' as a WCW executive. I didn't look down on her, nor did I think any less of her, really – I just felt bad for her. I could see how the people around her – including Vince Russo – manipulated the way ideas were presented to her, or obscured the real motivation behind those ideas.

In the years leading up to Hulk's arrival, Dixie had signed a sizable number of other big-name talent, including Sting, Kevin Nash, Mick Foley, Kurt Angle, and Booker T. Soon, in addition to the short-lived involvement of Scott Hall and Sean Waltman, Ric Flair, Jeff Hardy, Rob Van Dam and Ken Anderson would be added to the roster as well. It was almost tempting to believe that these signings were somehow strategic in nature, or perhaps part of some wider plan related to growing the business.

That wasn't the case – at all. Once I started having more and more conversations with Dixie, I really wanted to get a feel for what her vision was. I wanted to know what TNA planned on doing to make themselves unique. I wanted to understand how exactly the company was going to differentiate itself from WWE (being 'WWE Lite' was not an acceptable proposition).

As far as I could tell, however, the vision appeared to be something like, 'We're a wrestling company and I wanna be the next Vince McMahon.'

Not exactly what I was hoping for.

On October 27th, 2009, TNA and Spike TV, its television partner, announced Hulk's signing at a New York City press conference. A company press release detailed the particulars, including the role that Jason and I would have with BHE:

NEW YORK, Oct. 27 -- "Hulkamania" is back! The biggest name in professional wrestling history, Hulk Hogan, is joining Total Non-Stop Action Wrestling (TNA), the fastest rising wrestling organization in the world, and home to one of cable television's highest rated shows for young men, "TNA iMPACT!"

..."Hulk Hogan is one of the world's top pop culture icons and the biggest superstar in the history of professional wrestling. We are truly excited to welcome him into the TNA family," said Dixie Carter, President of TNA Wrestling. "Our goal is to become the world's biggest professional wrestling company. Hulk defines professional wrestling and we look forward to partnering with him in a variety of ways as we continue to grow TNA globally."

"I'm thrilled to be jumping back into the world of professional wrestling," said Hogan. "My fans have been asking me to return to the business for many years on a full-time basis, but the timing or the opportunity has never been right until now. TNA Wrestling is a great company with an already excellent fan base, business and broadcast partner. I firmly believe now is the time for some change at TNA as they are positioned to jump to the next level in their development and I'm here to work with Dixie to help make that a reality."

Through Hogan's partnership with Bischoff Hervey Entertainment Television, the deal with TNA was negotiated by longtime Hogan colleague Eric Bischoff. Additionally, BHE TV has inked a first-look deal with TNA and will be working with the organization to develop new programming extensions of the TNA brand.

"Hulk Hogan adds yet another level of star power that positions TNA iMPACT as Spike TV's version of 'Must-See TV' on Thursday nights," said Kevin Kay, president of Spike.

The announcement was made at a venue owned by Madison Square Garden - a not-so-coincidental shot at WWE (headquartered in Stamford, CT), for whom the Garden holds historical importance. I wasn't part of the discussions about where to deliver the announcement, by the way, but I thought it was a smart move regardless. From a promotional standpoint, it allowed TNA to say, essentially, 'The big announcement – coming at you from Madison Square Garden,' even if we weren't at the actual Garden, *per se*.

To this day, WWE produces events at Madison Square Garden that *lose* money for the company – even when they sell out. Why? Well, it's really frickin' expensive to book MSG as a venue. So why do it? The *perception*. The branding opportunities – particularly in the world of media and advertising. You can convert all of that into a financial windfall – if you do it right.

As I remember it, our announcement was more akin to a celebration. The rose had just begun to bloom, so to speak, and there was no angst, politics or negativity to be seen. Kevin Kay, the President of Spike TV, had been in attendance for the announcement, as had Scott Fishman, the production liaison between the network and TNA. Clearly, their network was fully on board with creating the perception of *competition*, relative to TNA's positioning and its opposition to WWE. There was perfect synergy between TNA and Spike in that respect.

Although it was not widely known at the time, it had been Spike, the *network* – and not TNA, the company - that footed the bill for Hulk Hogan's contract (the same can be said for Sting, Kurt Angle and some other top talent). TNA didn't have the budget for those high-priced contracts, and the Carter family, in my opinion, were not going to invest that much themselves. As a matter of record, Spike TV paid for Bischoff-Hervey Entertainment's deal as well.

I certainly can't speak for them, but it stands to reason that Spike's executives wanted to *compete* with WWE, based on their investments made in that high equity, nationally known talent. They wanted higher ratings. They wanted to be perceived as a bigger television property. They wanted to attract larger advertisers at higher rates. All of those factors would incentivize them to create a perception that TNA was not this little, regional, Nashville-based wrestling company that could only draw 200 people to a live event – but rather a legitimate, viable sports entertainment property.

Let's also be real for a minute. The moment that you bring in Hulk Hogan – and, to a lesser extent, Eric Bischoff – the narrative is always going to be, 'Wow, they're coming after WWE.'

We didn't do anything to discourage that narrative, and, in fact, we probably did a lot of things to encourage it.

Before we embarked on Hulk's TNA debut, there was some other business to attend to – specifically in Australia.

Hulkamania: Let The Battle Begin was a tour that ran in Melbourne, Perth, Brisbane and Sydney throughout November 2009, featuring the first wrestling appearance of Hogan in Australia (and, in the role of his opponent in the main event each night, the in-ring return of

59

Ric Flair).

The opportunity arose after I was contacted by the William Morris Agency - the talent agency that represented Jason and I in our business with BHE. I was introduced to Reno Anoa'i – *aka* Black Pearl of the famous Anoa'i wrestling family – who was running a training facility in Los Angeles. Reno explained that he had contact with a couple of legitimate, well-funded promoters in Australia (if memory serves me correctly, the promoters had even put on a *Rolling Stones* tour at one point), and therefore, he pitched the idea of constructing – with Hulk Hogan at the top of the card – a series of events *down under*.

Reno indicated that he could fill out part of the card, and for the other matches, it was no surprise that Hulk wanted to be surrounded with as many familiar faces as possible. While he still wanted to stay connected to the business – and this tour presented him with another such opportunity – Hulk wanted to feel at home with the group we selected. As such, the tour ended up including a mix of established stars, such as The Nasty Boys and Brutus Beefcake, with an array of newer talent including Ken Anderson and Orlando Jordan.

In every facet, the promoters tried to do a great job. The talent stayed in first-class hotels, and the events played in some of the largest venues in Australia. They definitely weren't cheap, but at the same time, the promoters may have overestimated things a little bit. Their expectations – relative to the kind of turnout that the tour would get – ended up being a little out of whack.

From a financial point of view, the tour failed to be successful – and that created a lot of challenges. We found ourselves in a little bit of a fight to get the money that was due to us, although ultimately, we did. More importantly, being able to travel to Australia – in consideration of the fans and the actual events themselves – added up to be a wonderful experience.

I'll never forget this story. Right before our first show with TNA, Dixie was hosting a Christmas party at her home in Nashville. I was still wide-eyed at this time, trying to be open-minded about the opportunity, and happy that the deal was finally done. When Dixie invited me to the party, I didn't give it any second thought: *Sure! Why not?*

Loree and I quickly hopped on a plane to Nashville, and soon we found ourselves inside Dixie's beautiful home. She had the event catered; the atmosphere was great – it was just a wonderful experience for most of the night. After we settled in a little, someone who introduced himself as an attorney for Panda Energy approached me. I thought we were having a conversation at first, but before long, I started to feel as if I was interviewing for a job. It definitely wasn't the kind of interaction one would expect at a Christmas party.

In any event, I had soon forgotten about our little exchange – that is, until Dixie approached me about two weeks later. *Eric*, she said with a concerned look on her face, *what did you say at my Christmas party?*

Clearly, her question was in reference to my discussion with the Panda lawyer. *We just chatted for about ten minutes*, I shrugged.

I don't think I said anything to him that mattered.

Her reply was as puzzling as the subject itself.

Well, Eric, she said.

That's not what we've heard.

61

Now I was *really* confused. The tone of my response was of genuine astonishment: *What exactly did you hear, Dixie?*

Evidently, word had 'gotten back' to Dixie – along with Bob and Janice Carter, by the way – that I had bad-mouthed Dixie, TNA and the entire operation during my little summit with the Panda guy.

During the party, Loree had been by my side the entire time. With that in mind, I asked Dixie if she believed that I'd get into *any* kind of business discussion – in the middle of a Christmas party (!), no less – as my wife and I were enjoying a cocktail in Dixie's home. *Wouldn't that be particularly strange*, I asked rhetorically, *if I was also speaking to someone who I didn't know?*

I didn't really get a response.

It was all so bizarre.

The Move to Monday

7

One of the things that TNA suffered from – badly – was a general lack of awareness. Throughout 2009, its flagship show on Spike, *Impact*, averaged 1.5 million viewers per episode – cause for celebration in 2022, perhaps, but barely a blip back then. We needed to do something to create more awareness, to create more *controversy* – to coin a phrase.

To that end, I was a pretty loud voice in advocating that Hulk's debut occur on a *Monday* night, and not on a Thursday night, the typical *Impact* time slot. TNA had cultivated a nice little choir who they preached to each and every Thursday, but there was no 'noise' outside of that. Outside of their small audience – again, relative to that time – there was zero awareness that TNA even existed.

I thought, 'Okay – you're making a big move here. You're bringing in Hulk Hogan, for God's sake. There's nothing you could do that's bigger than that. Rather than doing it on a Thursday night – just for the choir in your church – let's turn shit upside down. Let's make a big noise.'

Going on a Monday night, of course, meant going *head-to-head* with WWE and *Monday Night Raw*, as per the famous ratings battles of the *Monday Night Wars* era. *Raw* had averaged over 5 million viewers throughout 2009, but strategically, the competition was certain to create a huge buzz – and one that TNA could not afford otherwise. Spike was fully behind the move, too, and subsequently, preparations began for Hulk's debut episode of *Impact*: Monday, January 4th 2010.

Part of those preparations involved sitting down for a discussion with Russo. Dixie had wanted me to 'clear the air' with him before we started working together – a suggestion that at that time, I was willing to go along with. For his part, Russo tried – in his own way – to apologize for what had happened in the past. In return, I took his apology as sincere – he wasn't lying, as far as I could tell, or trying to manipulate me once we started talking.

In his own words, Russo discussed being 'born again', having found his faith in Christ since we had last worked together. Based on the way that he was conducting himself, I could tell that Russo was thinking about that a lot. He was attempting to overcome, in my opinion, a lot of the baggage that *he* brought to the table, and again, I took that attempt as sincere.

Now don't get me wrong – I was never going to have blind faith or trust in Russo ever again. I knew exactly what he was capable of. At the same time, there was no way that he was going to *get me* again, and so if we had to work together, I thought, 'We can still have a positive working relationship.'

I decided to let Russo know that I wasn't going to be holding a grudge. I wasn't going to let what happened ten years ago get in the way of what was in front of us. I essentially outlined what our options were: *we have two choices here. We can either work together to make sure it doesn't work, or we can work together to make sure it does.*

Let's make it work.

With that aside, it was time to let the world know about the move to Monday. On December 5th, Dixie, Hulk and I appeared on the finale of *Spike*'s *The Ultimate Fighter*, its UFC-produced reality show, and in a cage side interview with Joe Rogan, Hulk delivered the news to the audience at home:

We just got the green light, brother. On January 4th, TNA Impact...we're going wide open. We're going head-on-head. We're going to battle with the WWE. Monday night, January 4th...Hulk Hogan and TNA...we're coming after everybody.

Once January 4th arrived, *Impact* was set to air unopposed for the first hour (8-9pm EST), and head-to-head with *Raw* for the final two hours (9-11pm EST). We formatted the show so that Hulk would make his entrance to the *Impact Zone* – aka soundstage 21 at Universal Studios Florida, where *Impact* was broadcast from – just in time for *Raw* to go live at 9pm. After making his entrance, Hulk took to the microphone and signaled the arrival of a new era:

There is so much talent in the back – so many young guys that are runnin' so hard. And yes, guys...there's a lot of old faces in the back that are ready to gear up. TNA is gonna be the number one company in the world.

Hulk was quickly interrupted, as per the show format, by the arrival of Scott Hall, Sean Waltman, and – rounding out the nWo reunion – Kevin Nash. Soon I made my own entrance, proceeding to make reference to our shared history together:

It's been a while, hasn't it? Brings back memories, doesn't it? I mean, look around you. In this ring right now are the guys that reinvented this business. We took on the 800-pound gorilla and we put him in a little monkey cage, and we spanked him! In the process, we changed this business forever.

...The team of Hogan and Bischoff have done it before, and I'm damn well sure we can do it in TNA, 'cause there's a whole lot of talent – great talent in the back

– and there's a whole lot of heart in this company. We're gonna take it to the very top.

As an on-screen pairing, the tag-team of Hulk and I still had value. Based on our history together, we still resonated with the audience, and although I wasn't excited about being on camera again, it was another effort to create credibility in what TNA was doing. It helped fuel the perception that TNA was making a big move - that the company wanted to compete on a major level.

Hulk ended his promo with another warning shot from the ring:

The change starts tonight. From the moment we got here, we started shuffling the deck. Things aren't gonna change until we conquer, become the number one sports entertainment company in the world…and the change will keep on going, until we're on top of the mountain!

…If you can't talk, and you can't wrestle, pack your bags and head up north!

In a post-show press conference, Dixie related to reporters what Spike's expectations were for the ratings. "The network will be happy," she revealed, "if we hold the number we traditionally get on Thursday night. [Spike] would consider that a huge success."

Once the viewing figures actually came in, it was clear that our strategy had not only been successful, but, in fact, we had far surpassed the typical Thursday night audience. For the special Monday night show, *Impact* delivered an average of 2.2 million viewers – in head-to-head competition for two of its three hours – with a peak of 2.9 million viewers for the Hulk Hogan debut segment (concurrently on the USA Network, *Raw* featured, in direct opposition, a long-awaited showdown between Bret Hart and Shawn Michaels).

The move had achieved its desired effect. We created a buzz. We preached outside our little choir. We let the world know that there was something other than WWE on television. While granted, the opposing episode of *Raw* delivered an average of 5.6 million viewers, we had already achieved the highest televised audience in the history of *Impact*, beating the previous record of 1.97 million.

Furthermore, the *replay* of *Impact* - broadcast in its usual Thursday slot on Thursday 7th - attracted 1.3 million viewers, further demonstrating that our approach had worked.

In terms of the creative process, everything was running as smoothly as it could. The dynamic was still new – it was all very positive – and no-one disagreed with what Hulk and I wanted to do (as it related to his character). It was actually a fun experience at first. Russo would typically work with his team - including Ed Ferrera, for a short period of time anyway, and also a young man named Matt Conway, who doesn't get a lot of ink (he prefers it that way) – in order to get started on generating ideas.

I thought very highly of Matt. He was very young – I think he started as an intern at the company – but he was a very bright person with great creative instincts. I particularly liked that he wasn't easily swayed by people with more experience than he had. In addition to suggesting his own ideas, he was adept at structuring some of the *other* ideas that floated around the writing room (so as to make them viable for producing television). He made sure that all of the details were taken care of – continuity issues, and things of that nature. He was exceptional at that.

Typically, for about a week, Russo, Ed and Matt would work on the show together. I would then fly in to meet with them – and we'd run through the entire format. I would lay out a general direction for Hulk - mostly related to the tone and tenor of his character, as opposed to what he might do or say on-screen. Occasionally, I would also make suggestions about some other aspects, mostly related to the general flow of the show, for example. But for the most part, the process was simple: I would come in, look at what Russo and his team had, and then make the necessary changes.

Hulk gave his own description of the process in a radio interview:

I'll tell you how it works. Eric gets an overview of the shit and then Eric fixes everything.

There was no tension involved in that process. Russo knew that he couldn't 'throw down' - nor could he make a stand. I've never talked to him about it, but there was definitely a sense of, 'Okay – this train is leaving the station. It's going to this destination, and you can either get on the train or go home.'

With that in mind, Russo was pretty supportive and flexible in the beginning. I even found myself praising him in some public comments:

I work closely with Vince Russo. I see the formats…I give my suggestions. Vince and I have a great working relationship, and in regards to chemistry, I would say that besides my partner Jason Hervey and Hulk, there's no one better that I have a working relationship with.

Maybe hell was freezing over.

In comments made to *Multichannel News*, Kevin Kay, the President of Spike, indicated that he was open to making Mondays a more permanent home for *Impact*. "If it's successful," he was quoted as saying before the first show, "I'm not opposed to moving it to Monday nights. This is the time for this…TNA has a lot of momentum with Hulk Hogan and we have the ability to market and promote it."

For whatever the critics may have thought about January 4th, we had delivered over two million viewers on average that night – head-to-head with *Monday Night Raw*. Therefore, it became a natural conversation for us all to say, 'Wait a minute. It worked...so what if we went head-to-head again?"

Head-to-head competition – and the controversy and buzz that it created – helped launch WCW into the stratosphere. Within 12 months of *Nitro* going on the air, we were comfortably winning the *Monday Night Wars*; therefore, in that respect, directly challenging WWE, the industry leader, was a formula I already had success with. Now that we were in TNA, the formula had seemed to work again for the Monday in which we had premiered Hulk Hogan.

It was a natural progression, relative to the conversations that Spike and TNA were already having, to consider whether the Monday move should be permanent. I was a big part of those conversations – just for the record.

It wasn't my decision, but when the subject came up, I was *the* most enthusiastic person in the room.

For Every Action...

8

It all felt a little like history repeating. In the weeks following January 4th, the momentum was with us at TNA. We had Hulk Hogan. We delivered a record audience for *Impact*. We attracted an average of over two million viewers – while competing directly with WWE in the process. At the time I thought, 'Why would we *not* want to do this on a regular basis?'

I found myself saying as much in a contemporaneous interview:

> It's a little bit of history repeating itself. This is a great opportunity for TNA to step up and get noticed, to showcase their product. I've said since the moment I started talking to Dixie, in my opinion, that we should go head-to-head with *Monday Night Raw*. To me, it's a battlefield – and to win the battle, you have to be on the battlefield.

Any of the initial expectations for Hulk's debut had far been exceeded by the initial ratings response; however, it was during the subsequent weeks of TNA programming that our momentum started to dwindle. Quite frankly, the overall quality of *Impact* didn't really change, and to those more accustomed to a WWE-type presentation, TNA still felt more like a *game show* (by virtue of its location at the Universal soundstage) as opposed to a live action wrestling event.

Furthermore, we had another challenge to overcome: if TNA was to go head-to-head permanently, such a programming change could not be made immediately. Contrary to what some on the periphery of the wrestling business may believe, a television network can't just make a programming change of that magnitude overnight. There are a ton of decisions and logistical considerations that first have to be worked out – in short, there would *have* to be delay.

Despite the narrative that may suggest otherwise, I was never aware of any discussions regarding Spike's expectations for the Monday experiment. To be clear, there were no parameters that we had to reach – no-one from Spike said, 'Okay, we're going to try this, but unless you achieve 'x', you're done' – those kinds of conversations never took place. Nonetheless, by the time *Impact* eventually moved to its new Monday time slot (March 8th), our momentum had stalled to the point where the show drew a .98 rating - representing 1.4 million viewers – whereas in opposition, *Raw* attracted a 3.4 rating (and 5.1 million viewers). *Impact* then drew a .84 rating on March 15th (with *Raw* improving to a 3.7) before soon falling to a .62 on March 29th (in opposition to *Raw's* 3.7).

Given the number of people who had sampled the first offering on January 4th, there was a certain level of disappointment at the *level* of audience loss (*Impact* eventually bottomed out with a 0.5 rating on April 26th), and as the numbers deteriorated, Spike started to become more concerned. They started to look at the situation like, 'Okay, what else can we do to reclaim this momentum? How do we build it back? What's the strategy going forward?'

Unfortunately, *there was no strategy*. Oh, there was a *short-term* willingness – on the part of TNA – to say, 'Let's go ahead and see what happens', but there was no plan after that. There was no plan to take the show on the road. There was no plan to improve the quality of the product – at least beyond bringing in the latest big name.

Creating momentum is easy, but *sustaining* momentum is ten times harder. Spike was willing to commit to a long-term strategy – provided that TNA and its staff understood the meaning of the phrase – but there was only so much that the network could do.

While Spike was elated at the beginning, there was only *so much* promotion they could realistically afford. Furthermore – although some in TNA seemingly failed to realize this – Spike had a variety of *other* shows that required adequate promotion on their network. It was up to TNA to demonstrate what the vision was – and that's where the rubber, so to speak, left the fucking road.

On May 3rd, Spike announced that effective May 13th, *Impact* was moving back to its Thursday time slot. "The fans have spoken and with their input," announced Brian Diamond, Spike TV's Senior Vice President of Sports and Specials, "we have determined the best time slot to maximize the TNA audience is on Thursday nights…where we are confident it will be among the most-watched shows with young men."

"Our fans made it clear that they preferred the Thursday night time period," added Dixie. "By moving to Thursdays, this is a win-win opportunity for both TNA and its fans. We are looking forward to delivering what the fans are asking for."

For all of TNA's shortcomings – and the consequential effect on our ability to compete with WWE – Hulk and I received our fair share of criticism, too. Many of the TNA 'die-hards' resented the fact that we surrounded Hulk with a lot of the names he had been surrounded with in the past – The Nasty Boys, for example – and in large part, I think that criticism was fair.

I didn't want to rely on the late '90s audience – or even the mid-to-late '80s audience – I wanted to present TNA in a new, fresher way. By surrounding Hulk with people like the Nasty Boys, it was my belief that we were going 'back to the future' in the worst possible manner. Jimmy Hart was another character that I was determined to keep off television.

While I don't know this for sure, I think Dixie felt similarly, but she was willing to give Hulk that flexibility – in order for him to do what he believed needed to be done. No judgments there, by the way – I faced the same kind of situation in WCW, and I've been there and done that when it comes to dealing with talent. While critics will sit there and say, 'I wouldn't entertain *any* concessions from talent,' or, 'I would just send them all home,' the reality is that concessions *do* have to be made – much in the same way that a movie studio has to make concessions to certain directors or talent.

It's all part of the game – and sometimes it works out great (sometimes it doesn't). In this particular case, Hulk had leverage – and he believed that certain talents were still viable on television.

Another frequent criticism surrounded Hulk's decision to get back in the ring (the March 8th *Impact* featured a tag-team match involving Hulk, Abyss, Ric Flair and AJ Styles). For the record, I wasn't supportive of it – and I expressed my feelings to Hulk in the most constructive way possible.

Although it was a conversation that Hulk and I have had many, many times – even going back to the late '90s – it remained a *difficult* discussion. How do you tell Hulk Hogan that he can't perform in the ring anymore - at least to a level that he would be proud of?

There's a reason why the Rolling Stones still tour to this day – and it's not because they need the money. It's not even really because of their egos.

It's because of their love of performing – it's who they are. It's what they do. It's their identity – and the same is true with top-level wrestlers. It's one of the reasons why Ric Flair came out of retirement to wrestle for TNA, too – he's *become* Ric Flair at this

74

point (as opposed to Richard Fliehr, his birth name). He's been 'The Nature Boy' for the majority of his life.

Hulk wanted so badly to go out and be the Hulk Hogan he had always been – to connect with the audience in a unique and special way. It was a strong, compelling emotion for him, but I didn't want to see him go out and be *less* than the memory that people had previously. That was my biggest concern, but Hulk felt too strongly about it. Once he made up his mind, it was my job – as a producer and as his friend – to mitigate the risks as much as possible.

It wasn't feasible for Hulk to have a 15-minute match, or to go back in time to some of the things he did in the '80s and '90s. I used to tell him instead, 'Hulk, they want to see three things. They want to see a pose. They want to see you cup your ear. They want to see you throw that big right hand – and that's all you need to do!'

'You don't need to do the leg drop,' I would say, 'And you don't need to prove that you're still capable of having a 'great match'. You need to go out and just be Hulk Hogan!'

I suppose it was my 'less is more' strategy, but with Hulk – like anyone else who's been such a powerful performer (and there aren't many of them) – it's like trying to slow down a racehorse. That racehorse is going to run as fast and as long as it can – regardless of whether it's competitive any longer.

That's just instinct – and the same was true with Hulk.

With that being said, perhaps the stupidest form of criticism related to a change that we made before the short-lived move to Mondays. For six years, TNA had been producing its matches inside of a *six-sided* ring – as opposed to the typical four-sided ring – until we nixed the idea as soon as possible.

I don't care what anyone says – the six-sided ring was stupid. When I inquired about the logic of the idea, the response would be something like, 'When people are flipping through the channels, they're gonna see that six-sided ring and stop!'

First of all – as of 2010 – people weren't 'clicking through the channels' to the same degree that they had been previously. Therefore, that sounds like an absurd strategy – to build an audience because people are 'clicking through the channels.'

What the fuck?

Secondly, the six-sided ring presented a big challenge for the talent in the ring – and for the viewer, it added nothing.

Nonetheless, everybody in the TNA office felt like it was their *identity*.

No – it was dumb as shit.

If your one branding statement was a six-sided ring, that's fucking stupid.

I was just as disappointed as anyone else about the failed move to Mondays. Prior to the decision, I had great confidence in going head-to-head with WWE – mostly because it was a strategy that had worked for me in the past. In retrospect, I can now see that while we had great success with the same approach in WCW, there was one key difference: our company had the long-term support of its ownership (that being TBS, Inc. at the time of *Nitro's* premiere).

Fast forward to 2010, and I wish the older, wiser me would have said, 'Yeah, but Eric, if you don't have the long-term support behind you, it's not going to work.' Now, don't get me wrong: on the *network* side, we had just about as perfect of a situation as one could hope for. I wouldn't go as far as to say that Spike *loved* the head-to-head idea - but they liked the idea. They were nervous about it - and they should have been, because it was a big, bold, loud move – but there wasn't a lot of push back on their end. There was *support* from Spike. The conversations were more along the lines of, 'Okay – if we're going to do this – what can we do to help you from the network side?'

I think Dixie was excited about the *potential* of the move being successful, but again, without a long-term plan or long-term support – so that you weren't living and dying with what happened *today* – it just wasn't going to work. Sometimes you win on a daily basis - and something you lose on a daily basis - but if you're marching towards a destination, you take those wins (and those losses) and you keep on marching anyway.

You keep on marching - *if* you have a long-term vision and the necessary support behind you.

I didn't know it at the time, but we had no real long-term support or commitment from TNA's funding partner. Internally, management was, as a collective group, more focused on 'What did we do today?' or 'How much money did we make in merch sales?'

When you have that kind of short-term mentality, a long-term plan is bound to fail, and eventually, that's what happened.

One of the first things I noticed – almost immediately upon my arrival to TNA – was the undercurrent of negativity that existed towards Spike. There seemed to be a kind of 'us versus them' mentality, possibly because everybody realized that Spike had the 'keys to the car', relative to TNA's continued viability as a television product.

In television, *he who writes the check writes the rules* – that's just how it is. For some reason at TNA, there was a resentment towards the fact that Spike – as is typical for any television network – possessed the ability to pick up the phone and ask for answers to certain questions, or simply offer suggestions of their own. It wasn't so much of a problem for Dixie – she was naturally smooth in managing those kinds of situations – but it was for the people *around* her (particularly TNA's funding partners).

Certain people didn't seem to understand that in television, you have to recognize your television partner as a *client*. You're not doing them a favor by putting your show on their network – they're doing *you* the favor because they're writing the check! One of the things that I brought to the table was a different perspective on how to manage that relationship.

That perspective led to a series of conversations that I had with Kevin Kay and Scott Fishman, specifically around the possibility of adding a *second* show – not a wrestling show, *per se*, but a reality-based show involving some of our talent.

Dixie was enamored with the reality television business, and at times, it seemed like she wanted to be in that business herself. With her support, Jason and I started exploring different ideas, but it soon became clear that the potential budget was an issue. In addition to spending a ton of money on the *Impact* show – simply from a licensing fee perspective – Spike, as stated, were also footing the bill for a number of TNA's top stars. Therefore, in a conference call with Kevin and Scott, I suggested the idea – based on the fact that we would already be on location – to film the second show concurrently. It was an economy of scale solution as much as a creative concept.

One of the things that's missing in our show, I explained, *is the ability for the audience to feel like they're getting to know the characters.*

What if – once the show is over – we sit the talent down and get their reactions to what just happened on the main show. We'll basically be recording 'confessional' type interviews with them – similar to what Jason and I do with our reality shows.

They'll be a sit-down interview, for example, with one of the principals involved in a particular angle. As we roll the footage of what just happened, that person – or that group of people – will be telling the audience what they were really thinking as that event unfolded.

The show will be about presenting reactions from people who are featured on the main show – including talent who we don't get to hear from on a regular basis.

Everyone loved the concept of *TNA Reaction,* as we eventually decided to call it – but there was still one problem. Spike were not too crazy about funding the show – they were kind of tapped out for the time being – but then again, therein lied an opportunity. Forced to consider the most cost-effective way to produce the new show, Jason and I went to TNA and said, 'For an additional $15,000 per week...' – that's how much it would cost to make it suitable for television – '...we can do this ourselves.'

For Jason and I, the additional payment was incremental to our existing agreement with TNA. But it wasn't really about the money – I just wanted *control* over the project. Nobody in TNA had a handle on how to produce the documentary-style show that we were proposing. They didn't know how to shoot it – nor did they know how to edit it.

The format for *Reaction* was much different to what professional wrestling fans were used to. The show delved much more into the characters, story and psychology behind many of the on-screen feuds. Another aspect that made *Reaction* unique was that we shot it on a medium that was relatively new to television – DSLR (Digital Single Lens Reflex) video. The result was a highly compressed, grainy video output (by virtue of the frame rate) that contrasted sharply with what TNA (and WWE) had done previously.

The show was both a critical and financial success. All of a sudden, we were providing a wider range of talent with a spotlight to get over with the TNA audience. From a return-on-investment perspective, a show that was costing TNA $15,000-an hour to produce was delivering between 800,000-1,000,000 viewers per episode (the first edition of *Reaction* garnered a .87 rating, representing 1.14 million viewers).

Over time, one of the unintended consequences of the new format, however, was that it became watered down. Due to the positive response – from both talent and fans alike - there was a natural temptation to say, 'Why don't we make this 'look' part of the core show, too?'

As you do more of something – by definition – it no longer remains unique. But that wasn't the only challenge, as at the time, it was a very time-consuming process to transfer all of the footage shot on a DSLR camera – nothing like a traditional video camera where video could be shot (and edited) minutes before it aired. Once we started using the same techniques on *Impact*, we were forced to shoot the confessional-style interviews far in advance; if AJ Styles, for example, had a match that aired at 9 o'clock in the evening, we would have to shoot his interview at 3 o'clock in the afternoon (and then make it appear as though the interview was happening *after* the match – not an easy feat).

Nonetheless, the innovations that arose out of *Reaction* represented some of the highest points of my TNA tenure. I was at a restaurant in Nashville when I found myself reminded of the old axiom: *imitation is the sincerest form of flattery*. I looked up from my plate to glance at a television screen – only to notice that *Raw* had started to implement our new techniques.

They're stealing your shit, read a text from a friend of mine, followed by another.

Ah, I'm used to it, I responded.

They've been stealing my shit for a long time.

It was now about half a year since Hulk and I joined TNA, and I was starting to become much more involved in creative. Although my contract, as stated, was written in such a way to specifically outline the things that I would *not* get involved in (hiring, firing and anything relative to creative outside of Hulk), the creative process was starting to become *fun*.

Over the period of several months, I had developed, rather organically, a broader creative relationship with Vince Russo. I still didn't trust Russo, but the relationship was becoming more comfortable to me. I wasn't constantly watching every move he made – or listening carefully to every word he said – and consequently, I found myself getting more involved. I didn't want to 'call the shots' - or have final decision-making authority on anything, really – but my role was becoming more like a consultant, for lack of a better word.

For quite some time, I would fly into Nashville on a Monday night, meet up with Russo and his team on Tuesday, and *maybe* stick around on Wednesday before I was gone. It was kind of a rinse and repeat process for those first six months.

By mid-summer, however, I found myself actually *looking forward* to those creative meetings; of coming up with ideas and fine-tuning the ideas that had been presented to me. My enthusiasm continued to grow as we mapped out some long-term directions for storylines. I didn't raise my hand in order to get even *more* involved – I didn't ask for permission or anything like that – but gradually, I started to take more control.

By June, we were building everything towards *Bound For Glory* – yet four months away – with the development of the "10.10.10" angle (named as such due to the date of the event itself).

Bound For Glory promised to reveal the identity of "They" – a mystery that eventually led to the creation of *Immortal*. As part of an elaborate ruse, Hulk and I turned heel – at the Ocean Center in Daytona Beach, no less (the site of the nWo's formation in 1996) – alongside Jeff Hardy in a new heel role of his own. The following episode of *Impact* allowed me to explain that we had conned Dixie – in storyline, of course – in order to gain complete control over TNA:

What we did - normally, in the business world – would be considered a hostile takeover. In this case, it's not so much of a hostile takeover, as it was a work of art!

Rembrandt...Monet...couldn't come up with...couldn't conceive a piece of art as beautiful as what we did!

While the dirtsheets trashed TNA's latest on-screen development, the numbers told a different story. The post-*Bound For Glory* episode – with hardly any wrestling in the first hour, yet plenty of storyline development – attracted the highest audience since January.

Second Generation

9

O n November 7th, 2010, as part of the *Turning Point* pay-per-view, we debuted a new referee in the main event. The Jeff Hardy-Matt Morgan bout was officiated by Jackson James, a seemingly inexperienced ref with no prior trace on the independent scene.

What followed was an 11-month storyline that would eventually reveal, among other things, that 'Jackson' was in fact my son: Garett Bischoff.

Although as a youth, Garett had been *immersed* in professional wrestling - by virtue of my involvement in it - he had never once expressed an interest in getting involved himself.

Then one day, all of a sudden, he caught me by surprise with a question.

Dad, what can I do to break into the business?

I could only think of one reply: *Why the hell would you want to do that?*

I wanted to be supportive, but I also wanted to get into Garett's head - to understand his motivation in the first place. If I'm being completely honest, I was also trying to think of the best possible way to talk him *out* of it.

I really had no desire to see Garett get involved in the wrestling industry - for a number of reasons. First, I considered it my responsibility, as his father - and someone who had spent a lot of time in the industry - to give him a reality check, or at least get him to consider a different perspective.

The first thing I told him was: *Garett, here's the truth. Because you're my son, you have the opportunity to access people that will expedite the process – especially compared to someone off the street who doesn't know anybody in the wrestling business, or who doesn't have a parent at a fairly high level in the industry.*

I can shortcut a lot of the process, and so in that respect, being born a Bischoff is great news!

But - it comes with a burden.

From the day I walked into the wrestling business, I had *heat*. For a variety of reasons, I was always a polarizing figure – partially because I lacked credentials, to begin with. I didn't have any experience. I didn't train in a wrestling school. I didn't work on the independent scene, or as part of the territories like the majority of those in the business. I was just a guy who looked like the weather man at a small, local television station – a guy who ostensibly just walked into a high-profile position.

Add that to the fact that from the beginning, I always had a lot of visibility. Even during my time with the AWA, for example, I was hosting a show on ESPN every afternoon. To a segment of the audience, I think the general impression was something like, 'Who is this guy? Why did he even get this opportunity? He's horrible!'

As time went on – and my profile grew larger – a lot of that perception traveled with me. When I eventually became President of WCW, that kind of inherent, 'Why does *he* have this job?' mentality prevailed, too – albeit this time, on a much larger scale. Becoming an on-screen character - and in particular, putting myself in the nWo - only seemed to add fuel to that fire.

With that in mind, I told Garett that he may discover - should he decide to pursue wrestling as a career - that the *disadvantages* of carrying the Bischoff name may in fact outweigh the advantages. But even putting my personal history to the side, I had witnessed plenty of *second-generation* performers trying to break into the business, and typically, it didn't seem to go so well.

There's often an inherent disadvantage in being a second-generation performer in our industry. The audience has a tendency to say, 'Oh, he or she is only there because of their last name – they didn't really earn it.' It can result in a sense that the performer is being *handed* something – as opposed to actually *earning* something – and nobody likes the stench of nepotism.

Although not a wrestler, I had been a fairly high-profile talent with a polarizing perception, in some quarters at least, based on my previous successes and failures. Consequently, I knew that regardless of how hard Garett worked – and irrespective of whatever talent he had – there would be a stigma that would follow him. It would be something to this effect: 'Oh God, there's Eric Bischoff's son.'

I knew that not *everyone* would feel that way, but the loudest portion of the audience – the Internet wrestling community in particular – would immediately go on the offensive. I thought about Greg Gagne - an incredibly talented performer who learned from one of the best ever, his father Verne – and the reception that he got from some fans in the AWA. No matter how good some of Greg's matches were –

from a storytelling or psychological perspective – it simply didn't matter to a segment of the audience. All they did was look at him and shrug, 'Ah, that's *Verne's son.*'

To some degree, Garett would have the burden of 'following in his father's footsteps' – as if the wrestling business wasn't difficult enough! That level of pressure might be tough for the average person to comprehend, but then again, people who want to break into the wrestling business typically *aren't* average people. They're driven. They have a unique desire. They make a commitment that the average person wouldn't make – not only to learn the industry and hone their craft, but more importantly, to *compete* amongst some serious, high-level athletes.

A very, *very* small percentage of people who want to break into the entertainment business are ultimately able to make a career out of it – and wrestling is much the same. It's probably even *more* true in the case of the wrestling business; after all, only a relatively small group of people make a serious living in the industry at any given time (perhaps hundreds of people – not thousands or tens of thousands of people - contrary to perception).

As a kid, Garett had been around wrestling a lot, and both he and Montanna, my daughter, came to events with me as often as possible. When it was 'bring your kids to work day', for example, I remember how confident and outgoing they were in interacting with other people in the WCW offices. When we would go to the extended TV tapings at the Disney-MGM studios, Garett in particular loved being backstage – and 'cutting up' (as they say in the South) with various wrestlers on the roster. He was always screwing around with Rick Steiner, I remember – they loved playing practical jokes on each other, that sort of thing – and so being around the wrestlers was natural for Garett. At the same time, that in itself was kind of a 'Catch 22', in the sense that he hadn't seen the *journey* that those in the industry had taken to get there. It was all fun and games from a child's vantage point – but Garett was kept away, by necessity, from a lot of the chaos and adult conversations that happen in that space.

I wanted to bring the reality of the situation to the forefront of his mind.

Look at the industry right now, I mentioned to him one day.

(Now, keep in mind, this is at a time before the independent scene really started to heat up.)

There's really only one place to work, I told him, making reference to WWE - and not even thinking about TNA.

That's really only one place where you can actually have a career.

Not only do you have to do the same thing that everybody else does (i.e. breaking through the thousands of other hopefuls that want to be 'in the business'), *but you have to overcome the inherent challenge of being a second generation performer.*

You're going to have to commit five or ten years of your life for an opportunity to work for the one company that can realistically offer you a career.

In addition, I told Garett, there was the prospect of injury to contend with.

Even if you overcome the burden of your last name, I said, *and overcome the perception of nepotism that the audience may have towards you – and overcome the competitive nature of this industry*

– there's always a chance that an injury may take you out of the game anyway.

At the time, Garett was in a serious relationship with Mary Jane, with whom he later married. *Given the entirety of these circumstances*, I summarized, *it's not a great career choice!*

But let's say you overcome all of these challenges, I continued, looking at things from a different angle. *What about the lifestyle?*

In my experience, the hardest part about being successful in the wrestling business is related to the *lifestyle* that arises from one's participation in it. Putting aside the obvious vices and temptations – drugs and alcohol, most notably – wrestlers are away from home for hundreds of days per year. As a result, the majority of relationships involving wrestlers tend not to persist very long. *Imagine what it might be like*, I told Garett, *when you can only see your future child one or two days per week.*

By the way, I continued, *when you do see that child, you'll have precious few hours to adjust to being home – and to sleep enough that you have energy to enjoy it – before it's time to start packing to leave again.*

These kinds of realities have a really powerful and profound impact on a relationship – especially if the goal is to have a family, as was the case with Garett and Mary Jane. When Garett was growing up, although I worked many, many hours per week, I was at home at night – for the most part. If Garett wanted to pursue wrestling as an in-ring vocation, that would not be his experience at all.

It may read as if I was trying to *completely* discourage Garett from achieving his goal, but that's not entirely accurate. I was merely trying to paint a very realistic, honest and straightforward picture of what he would need to overcome in the business.

To Garett's credit, he listened, understood and was grateful for the advice.

He remained resolute regardless.

Over the course of the next month or two, we continued having variations of the same conversation, until one day, Garett came to me and said, 'Dad, I really, *really* want to do this.'

In my opinion, I had now done my job as his father. I had painted a realistic picture and reviewed all of the challenges that Garett would have to overcome. At this point – his commitment being obvious - it was time to figure out the best way forward.

If you really want to do this, Garett, I said, *here's how you do it. You jump in your car and you drive to Los Angeles. I have a pretty good relationship with Rikishi and some of the people at his wrestling school. I have a lot of respect for the people coming out of that school, and if you go there, he's not going to treat you like my son.*

He's going to treat you just like everybody else – and that's what you need.

Putting yourself through wrestling school – especially under the tutelage of Rikishi – isn't exactly a fun experience.

Now we'll find out, I thought to myself, *just how committed he really is.*

91

At the time – mainly because I was sick of staying in hotels so often – I had an apartment in Santa Monica (due to the success that Jason and I were having with BHE, I was visiting LA on a very regular basis). It was a small, two-bedroom place – right on the beach – and as my contribution, I let Garett stay there while he was at the school. He wasn't making a lot of money at the time, but he had a little bit of cash – and he used it all to support his dream, paying his way for the training and all of his other expenses.

Garett worked his ass off with Rikishi and by the end of the training, he had a pretty good handle on the fundamentals. But fundamentals aren't enough, and if I would have thrown Garett out in the ring back then, he would have gone up in flames in a matter of minutes. There would have been the obvious accusations of nepotism - of course - but more importantly, he was nowhere near ready for television.

It was time for the second step of the process.

I want you to come to Florida, I told Garett, *and you're gonna go train with Brian Knobbs.*

It might sound crazy to some people – because everybody has their opinion of him as a performer – but Brian Knobbs came up under Brad Rheingans, a former Greco-Roman, Olympic (1976 and 1980) and professional wrestler with experience both overseas in Japan, and domestically in the United States.

Many people who were successful in our industry were trained by Brad, who understood (and taught) wrestling psychology at a completely different level. Brad didn't just understand how to execute really cool moves – many people fall into that category – he could actually impart the knowledge of what makes a wrestling match *work*. As Brian was one of Brad's students, that told me everything I needed to know about Brian's pedigree as a trainer

92

(which again, has nothing to do with the way he wrestled as a character).

In television, it's the dialogue – and the visuals associated with it – that creates the necessary emotion on the part of the audience. In wrestling, the *physical dialogue* that comprises great matches is how wrestlers tell *their* story. As far as I'm concerned, the ring itself is essentially a giant stage – and that's how wrestlers should look at it. Brian helped Garett learn a lot in that regard.

As Hulk and Brian were close at the time, Hulk naturally became interested in working with Garett – and teaching him how to become a *character* specifically. One day, I looked at Garett working with Hulk and said, 'Wow – he's put in the time learning the fundamentals with Rikishi. He's learning the psychology of wrestling with Brian, and now Hulk is teaching him how to present his character.'

While at the beginning, I had been pretty hard on Garett's ambition, by now I was *impressed* – he was doing a really great job. The next step, as far as I was concerned, was for him to gain experience as a *referee* – allowing him to perform on camera without the spotlight of being an in-ring wrestler. As a referee, he would have the chance to listen to wrestlers 'laying out' their matches backstage - being a fly on the wall, essentially, for conversations involving some of the biggest names in the history of the business. To a degree, he would also be earning his eventual spot as a wrestler, *paying his dues* in a far less glamorous (but highly essential) role instead. TNA ended up hiring him for that purpose.

When we show up at a TV taping, I instructed Garett, *don't even make eye contact with me. If you see me sitting down with Hulk or anybody else, don't join us. You have to keep yourself as far away from me as you can. Just be a part of the crew.*

93

For the longest time, there were a sizable number of people in TNA who didn't know that Garett was my son. He was *Jackson James* – the new official who was also new to the business – and that's how everyone treated him.

He was now learning the fundamentals of *televised wrestling* – a completely different skill set than what it takes to be successful at a live event. As I wanted the audience to see him as *only* a referee (and not an eventual wrestler), I was sure to keep Garett away from exposing that plan. *If, in the course of a match, you get someone's hands laid on you*, I told him, *just imagine you're a big wet rag. When you hit the mat, that's where you stay. Sell your ass off – don't expose that you can actually take a bump!*

Fortunately for Garett and his tenure as a referee, he avoided participation in one of the biggest clusterfucks ever – March 13th, 2011, at *Victory Road*, to be exact, when TNA made headlines for all of the wrong reasons.

Victory Road was set to culminate in a match between Jeff Hardy, now the former TNA champion, and Sting, who had recently dethroned Hardy on an episode of *Impact* (Sting also happened to be one of Jeff's childhood heroes). When Hardy's entrance music played for the bout, however, he stumbled through the curtain and staggered down the entrance ramp, looking absolutely in *no condition to perform.*

At the time, it had been Jeff's 'MO' to get to Universal Studios – the site of the *Impact* tapings – 'check-in', and then go into hiding until he was needed to come out (either for an interview segment or a match). I don't know where he hid on the night of *Victory Road*, but it's probably safe to assume he was busy doing whatever drugs he brought with him.

94

When it was time for Jeff to go out, it seemingly took forever to find him. I made my way over to the 'Gorilla' position – the staging area just behind the entrance curtain – before witnessing that no-one was stopping what was about to take place. While waiting for someone to make a decision, I stood back and watched Jeff make his way through the curtain.

It can't go down like this, I thought.

Fuck it.

If nobody else is going to do anything…

Sting had no idea that Jeff was fucked up, and out of respect for Steve Borden (and simply as a professional more broadly), I didn't want to see Steve have a match with someone who was completely wasted. As there were no ideas coming from anybody else about how to intervene, I soon found *myself* walking out to the people – not knowing at all what I was going to do.

A thought crossed my mind; specifically, that maybe - in my heel character - I could knock out Jeff and have the ref call a disqualification. But that wouldn't work, I soon realized – we would need to reframe the match as a *no disqualification* contest (this last-minute change would provide cover to support why I was coming out in the first place). Therefore, I would have to improvise my intervention - via the means of cutting an off-the-cuff promo - in *real-time* (while simultaneously rewriting the main event). It would all have to occur as I shared the ring with Sting, Jeff and the referee.

"Slight change of plans here, ladies and gentleman," I interjected, microphone in hand, as I made my way down the entrance way.

"Slight change of plans," I repeated upon entering the ring.

"We had a little situation," I began - trying preemptively to make sense of what was to follow.

Making reference to Sting's recent return and defeat of Hardy on television (a development that in storyline, had only been made possible by "The Network"), I continued: "On March 3rd...

"...the network got involved in our business..."

As in storyline, Jeff and I were aligned at the time (Hardy was the centerpiece of our heel *Immortal* faction), I went over to shake his hand (with the microphone strategically placed behind my back). Unbeknownst to the viewing audience at home, I quickly delivered my instructions to him:

It's going to be a Stinger Splash, Scorpion Death Drop – and you're out of here.

Walking back to the middle of the ring, I switched back into character mode. "...And because Mr. Hardy was taken advantage of – in such a blatant way – I want you to know that I'm gonna be fair."

With that, I put the microphone behind my back again, extending my hand to Sting for a handshake (in reality, I was now in the position of telling *him* what was going on – while still making it look like it was 'part of the show'). The crowd couldn't hear what I was actually saying to Sting:

Take him out – I just called it.

In essence, my message was for Sting to hit Jeff with his finish – and as soon as possible, get the fuck out of there.

"Really – shake my hand," I motioned back towards Sting on the microphone. "I want you to know I'm gonna be fair.

"Alright – have it your way! In order to make this a level playing field, here's what we're gonna do...I had a chance to talk with Mr. Hogan...we decided to level the playing field...and since Mr. Hardy was unable to prepare for *you* on March 3rd, we got together with Mr. Hardy...[and] let him know that we we're gonna change this match...[and] add a little stipulation. We're gonna make it a no disqualification match. Mr. Hardy's been able to prepare for [it]. That's the way it is-"

With that, Sting knocked me out, and he and Jeff proceeded to have their 'match' – all 88 seconds of it.

It was a horrible position for Sting to be in – particularly at that stage of his career. As far as Jeff was concerned, it was just *sad* – and concerning – to witness how much his off-camera struggles were affecting him on-screen. For TNA, it was an embarrassing, unprofessional and shameful situation that reflected badly on the entire organization.

97

From Day One, An Outsider

10

In May 2011, it was announced that TNA's flagship program would be rebranded as *Impact Wrestling*, as detailed in a company press release:

> "While the name change is subtle, it is also very powerful. TNA is proud to be in the wrestling business, and not afraid to say it. And, to emphasize our commitment we have added the word 'wrestling' to our already well-known 'iMPACT!' brand," said TNA chief marketing officer Al Ovadia.

> TNA is also launching the tagline, "Wrestling Matters," a statement that reflects every aspect of TNA Wrestling, from program content to marketing to live events.

> "We wanted a branding initiative that was scalable and could extend across all platforms," added Ovadia. "We asked our fans what it was about professional wrestling that they found most compelling. We learned it was no single aspect, their passion for wrestling was all-consuming. Whether it's the in-ring action, backstage brawls, the feuds or classic dramatic conflict of good vs. evil, it's the entire experience that makes 'wrestling matter.'"

The now-famous (or perhaps infamous) rebranding effort started when Spike approached Dixie with the idea. As I recall, the goal of the campaign was – similar to the prior move to Monday nights - to create more awareness outside of the existing audience (and to reinforce the strength of the brand with the existing audience). A meeting was called by Kevin Kay, Scott Fishman, and an executive named Brian Diamond in order to discuss the concept.

In retrospect, this part of the story is really quite amazing to me. During the meeting, Kevin, Scott and Brian outlined their belief that not only was a strong rebranding campaign needed, but that Spike were willing to *fund the campaign* (to the tune of a million dollars of the network's money). A million dollars towards rebranding TNA!

At the risk of being redundant, everyone knew that TNA sounded like…well, tits and ass! It sounded like the acronym. For that reason, there remained a number of people who were uncomfortable with the name, and consequently, Spike wanted to invest both time and money into something more fitting.

First of all, it's not often that a network is willing to spend a million dollars of their own money in service of branding (or rebranding, in this case) a company that *they don't own*. Spike didn't have any equity in TNA – not even a percentage of it – but they were willing to do it regardless.

In our work as independent television producers, Jason and I had experience in begging, borrowing, and pleading networks to simply *promote* the shows that we had produced for them. Here – in this case – we had a network *coming to the producers* and saying, 'We'll take care of it.' It was a really unique situation.

Their presentation was extremely thorough. Spike wanted to look at everything down to the opening music – in fact, they wanted a musical *theme* for the brand. I remember Brian sending across selections of music that Spike were willing to license – pieces that would fit the new tagline (again, a Spike creation) of *Wrestling Matters*.

Prior to the meeting, Spike had conducted research that suggested that TNA's viewers wanted to see more *action* – and less 'gaga', or backstage silliness, for example. The network believed it was important to reinforce the *quality* of the wrestling, and henceforth,

Wrestling Matters was created as an all-encompassing branding statement.

There was a commitment to promoting – both inside and outside of the network – the message that *Impact Wrestling* was truly an *alternative* to WWE.

In the end, however - like almost everything else involving the company – it became political.

I was told, courtesy of someone who was very close to the situation, that Janice Carter *hated* the campaign. Allegedly, she was upset at Spike for coming up with the very idea, thinking that it didn't make any sense to begin with.

Number one, I thought to myself, *you don't know anything about wrestling!*

You don't know anything about the wrestling business – or the entertainment industry.

You weren't a part of the process, and you don't even understand why Spike came up with – and paid for – this entire campaign!

Spike came up with it solely for your brand's benefit – to increase the value of your company – and rather than saying, 'Thank you', you bitch about it!

The implementation ended up being clumsy, disjointed and confusing. Fans were unsure as to if TNA had retired the company name – in favor of *Impact Wrestling* – or if the television show had simply changed its title (the latter being accurate).

Among other things, it reinforced – once again – the fact that no-one in TNA understood the concept of working *with* a network; of developing and harnessing a collaborative relationship with Spike. *That* fact – more than anything else that was happening on-screen – would always, ultimately, be the limiting factor.

As of mid-2011, the Carter family had made a substantial investment in TNA – some 30 million dollars in total (or so I was led to believe). By now, I was starting to get more inquisitive about what their vision was for the company, and although I don't know *for sure* what was going on, here's what I *think* it was all about.

From my perspective, it was becoming increasingly apparent that the Carter family – particularly Bob Carter - had invested in TNA for one reason: to give Dixie, his daughter, a project of her own.

But it wasn't *just* a private investment on the part of the Carter family. To be specific, it was their *company* – Panda Energy – that made the investment, and consequently, there may have been some people that were not too happy about such a use of funds.

As far as those people were concerned, TNA wasn't their core business. They built nuclear power plants, for crying out loud – all over the world - so to take a big chunk of cash and invest in a wrestling company…I don't think that made a whole lot of sense to some people. In many respects, I completely understand that sentiment.

After a while, the *feeling* that I got – based on certain conversations that I was exposed to – told me what it was all about for the Carter family.

It was all about getting those 30 million dollars back.

Provided that the initial investment was returned to Panda, I think there was a *hope* (although I don't think a lot of thought was given to this part) that TNA could get to a point where it would become self-sustaining.

That's certainly a logical thought process – and a smart business decision to make – *if* you have some idea of how you're going to get there.

That's where things fell apart.

Therefore, when Dixie called me one day and said, 'Hey, there's gonna be a conference call with my mother, Janice… (to the best of my knowledge, Janice was mostly the one *overseeing* the investment in TNA)' - I threw a flag up on that one right away.

'My mother has some questions,' continued Dixie, 'and she'd like you to be on the call.'

No, I replied to Dixie, *I'm not doing that. Now you're asking me to get involved in the business of TNA, and I don't want to do that. If Janice has a creative question, I'm happy to jump on that call…but I do not want to be involved in any kind of internal business discussions.*

Dixie was *flabbergasted*. She couldn't believe that I didn't want to be on this conference call, based on the fact that Janice - and some of the other top TNA staff - were going to be on the line.

I didn't want anywhere near it.

Allow me to explain. Over the course of the previous year, I had been exposed to some of the people in the TNA offices. I would hear some of those people obsessing over the 'per cap' (i.e. per capita merchandise sales) from the latest house show, practically high-fiving themselves in the process. Their 'per cap' figure was supposedly twice as high as WWE, and to them, it was an indicator that TNA was setting the world on fire.

That's fantastic, I would say. *Congratulations, guys – really.*

Just one question for you: how many people were in the arena?

Everyone remembers what the TNA attendance figures were back then – pitiful. Unless the company put on a show in the UK – where TNA had a fantastic following – they couldn't draw flies if the talent rolled themselves in horseshit.

The reply would come back: *Uh...we had 200 people there last night.*

Wait a minute, I would think after getting the attendance figure. *You're running around like you just won a fucking Emmy – all because you've got a per cap merchandise figure of 15 dollars, whereas WWE averages 10 dollars a head?*

WWE has 25 thousand people in the arena – and you're drawing 200 – but don't worry, you've got a higher per cap than WWE!

Do you really think that's a win?

Oh, it was an indicator, all right – an indicator that the lack of knowledge, understanding, experience and instinct that existed in Dixie, actually permeated throughout the company. I realized that I couldn't help people like that. If their vision was so limited – if their

104

understanding of the 'business of the business' was so limited – I didn't want to get involved.

The scary part is this: they actually thought they knew what they were doing. They really believed that they were good at their jobs. When I would ask a question (e.g. *'You only had 200 people in the building. Shouldn't you be thinking about getting more people in the building?'*), I became a heretic for pointing out the obvious. They were too busy getting excited over $680 in 'merch' profit to understand anything about what I was saying.

Whatever TNA wanted to be was a mystery to me – and it remains a mystery to this day. The employees in the company office were probably very nice people, most likely smart - and possibly successful in other things they've done in their lives. But when I would see everybody spend half a day patting themselves on the back, or taking each other out to lunch to celebrate all of this great news, it was an indication to me that these people were *beyond* fish out of water.

They were flopping around in the desert – with no idea how to *find* water.

For all of the dysfunction, my role in TNA had continued to evolve over time – first from being strictly limited to Hulk's creative, to eventually being appointed Executive Producer of *Impact*. I can reasonably surmise that some people – most notably, Vince Russo – probably felt more and more threatened as I was given more responsibility.

Curiously, Russo was now in the habit of calling me with complaints about Dixie – and he was often on the verge of tears.

105

Bro, she's driving me crazy.

Bro, she wants to be an on-screen character, bro.

Bro…

I had the feeling that Russo was *playing both ends against the middle* – i.e., that he was telling Dixie the exact opposite of what he was telling me.

As time went on, I more frequently found myself calling 'bullshit' on some of Russo's 'creative' ideas – and this made him uncomfortable. He was no longer in a position – as had been the case before Hulk and I got to TNA – where he could go through a creative meeting without being challenged. As far as I was concerned, he was clearly bad-mouthing me to Dixie, so much so, in fact, that Dixie felt compelled to call me on the subject.

The call didn't help matters much; what started out as a conversation ended up with Dixie in tears - and me yelling down the other end of the phone.

I was pretty much *done* with it.

Then I got a call from Guy Blake – a super guy and an attorney with TNA – while I was out in my truck one day, shortly before the next set of television tapings.

You're coming to TV, Guy asked. *Right?*

Nah, I replied. *I'm not.*

It's not gonna be productive – this craziness is gonna carry over to TV.

Not wanting to see me breach my contract, Guy talked me off that particular cliff. He suggested a sit-down meeting to hash everything out – relative to the issues between Dixie, Russo and myself - as by this point, Dixie was barely even speaking to me.

Once we got to TV, Guy led the meeting, and as planned, we all laid our cards on the table. Russo did his best to spin his usual bullshit, but before long, it became apparent what he had been up to all along. He had, in fact, been playing both ends against the middle – trashing me to Dixie while simultaneously complaining to me about her - as confirmed by an impartial member of the creative team.

Unfortunately for Russo, this person had seen and heard *everything*.

Eric's right, he simply said when asked.

With that, Russo was demoted (but not before breaking down in tears in front of the room), and soon after, he eventually quit TNA altogether.

Over time, Guy continued to operate as a mediator between Dixie and I - in large part because he was able to see the bigger picture. He understood the personal politics that strained Dixie's relationships with the rest of her family. There was a ton of in-fighting, evidently, with respect to various other family members who were decidedly against the TNA investment.

It was all very jarring, strange and bizarre to learn about, but then again, TNA itself was a bizarre environment to work in – starting with the confusion around what *goal* (or set of goals) we were supposed to be working towards.

When it came to my interactions with management, the person that I dealt with primarily was Dean Broadhead, TNA's Chief Financial Officer. While indirectly, Dean may have reported – in dotted-line fashion – to Dixie, he *also* reported (as one would expect) to the Carter family. As it related to Dean's position, there was bound to be some inherent conflict - in my opinion – as while he was serving one master (getting the Carter family their money back), the actual business of TNA was concerned with serving a different set of masters – the audience and television network primarily. But Dean was duplicitous - a Hall of Fame talent when it came to doubletalk, really – as two-faced as one could get.

For whatever reason, Dean would always refer to himself as a "big supporter" of mine, and whenever I stepped in his office, he went out of his way to indicate that sentiment.

It was all bullshit.

I knew it was bullshit because as soon as I stepped *outside* of his office, he would bury me until the cows came home. That wasn't uncommon for a number of people who worked at TNA – just for the record.

What *was* somewhat uncommon was Dean's tendency to constantly try and impress himself on me. We could have been talking about the weather before the topic of conversation invariably circled back to *The Legend of Dean Broadhead*. It would somehow dovetail back into a story about how Dean was a fighter pilot in Vietnam – dropping napalm on villagers, that sort of thing – and what a bad-ass he generally was.

108

One day, we were casually talking in his office when Dean reached in his desk drawer, pulled out a gun and started wiping it down with a cloth. The point of the exercise, as far as I could tell, was presumably to demonstrate that he *had* a gun – and that he wanted me to know it.

Within moments, he proceeded to put the gun away and resume our conversation – as if nothing had ever happened.

Like I said – *bizarre*.

Another person who comes to mind is Andy Barton, one of TNA's long-time Executive Vice Presidents. Andy was a perfectly nice guy – probably very intelligent and talented at other things in his life – but he had *zero* understanding of the live event side of the business.

If you *know* you don't have any experience - but also *know* that you need to listen to people who've kind of been there and done that – that situation can be managed. That wasn't the case with Andy, however, nor was it the case with anybody in the TNA offices. Nobody knew what the hell they were doing, but at the same time, everybody realized they had a pretty sweet gig going. For that reason, they didn't want to hear *anything* that might expose their lack of understanding about the business.

There was kind of a jail food mentality within TNA management. The last thing any of them wanted was someone like Eric Bischoff, whose successes – and failures, might I add – could have been used to much greater effect. Rather than embracing someone with my background, they were scared to death of being exposed by someone who knew more than they did. Consequently, I was treated like an *outsider* – from day one.

Supposing that I would have participated in that conference call, I can *guarantee* that any opinions or suggestions that I made would have been twisted, turned and spun into some kind of narrative that made me the *bad guy*. In such an environment, there's no reason to even engage with that kind of mentality – it's completely unproductive.

Ultimately, TNA management looked at Eric Bischoff as a *necessary evil*. If they wanted Hulk, they would have to have me.

I was treated as such from the very beginning.

From an *on-camera* point of view, I'm often embarrassed by a lot of my time in TNA. I wasn't keeping myself in television shape, and when I look at it now, I find myself saying, 'Jeez – you could have lost 20 pounds, dude. You could have actually dressed like a character – at least a little more than you did.'

There *were* some highlights, though - especially once Garett and I engaged in an on-screen feud. I knew there would be a time in which we could surprise the audience – in a positive way – by 'paying off' what his tenure as an official had actually represented, in addition to providing the impetus for his transition from referee to wrestler. The big reveal came at *Bound for Glory* in October 2011, and I think it was pretty effective: a backstage camera caught us colluding in secret (i.e. discussing how we were going to screw over Hulk in his match against Sting), to which 'Jackson' responded:

I understand...Dad.

Besides working directly with Garett, there were a number of other people at TNA who I greatly enjoyed spending time with.

Christopher Daniels was one such example. Prior to my arrival in TNA, Chris was being presented as kind of a 'goth' character – there's certainly an audience for that – but the role seemed far too niche for someone of his talent.

I specifically remember pulling Chris aside one day and saying, 'Hey man, do you have a few minutes?'

I wanted to get into his head a little bit, to see what his thoughts were on the way that his character was being presented. It was striking to me that Chris was very open-minded - and completely unassuming in his interactions with me. I had a few general ideas about his character – and potentially where things could go – but he was so receptive that I thought, 'Wow – now *here's* someone that I can work with.'

Eventually, I ended up collaborating often with Chris – and his tag-team partner, Frankie Kazarian – on some of the most entertaining segments that TNA ever produced. I had a *blast* working with those guys – it was a true collaboration. I would often throw out an idea that they would shape in a way that suited their respective personalities. There was a lot of mutual respect there, and I'm happy to count both Daniels and Kazarian as friends to this day.

AJ Styles was another talent with whom I eventually developed a strong relationship. At first, AJ was tough – he's a strong personality to begin with – and Hulk and I both felt strongly about developing his character. AJ was long heralded for his amazing physical talent, but in fairness, he was often fairly rigid when it came to connecting with the audience otherwise.

At the beginning, we decided to make AJ the on-screen protégé of Ric Flair, and that was a really hard transition for AJ. He hated being in that spot, quite frankly – it was evident to all of us that he didn't want to be in the role. While AJ never did anything to offend or

111

disrespect me, I knew there was a level of tension that existed between him and I (and Hulk, for that matter). Nonetheless, he was a professional about it – and he did it anyway.

A certain portion of the audience may have despised the AJ-Flair pairing, and I would agree with the assessment that creatively, it just didn't work. However, I would also argue that by forcing AJ out of his comfort zone, he ultimately became a more well-rounded *performer*.

That became especially evident when AJ featured in a storyline involving Daniels, Kazarian (and Dixie) in the summer of 2012. We concocted this crazy scene where AJ - about as pure as the driven show in real life – apparently had a side piece…Dixie!

It was eventually revealed that AJ and Dixie were *not* having an affair; rather, they had been meeting in secret to help an addicted pregnant woman - Clare Lynch – overcome her various problems. I know, I know – I didn't think it was the greatest storyline in the world, either. Our audience certainly *hated* it, but AJ grew tremendously in that spot. Our relationship moved on from him saying, 'Okay, fine – I'll do it,' to 'Okay, that's good – but what if we do *this* instead?'

Chris Park – or Abyss – was another long-time TNA star who developed greatly throughout 2012. Chris was someone that you always wanted to be in the trenches with you – he was loyal, committed and about as unselfish as anybody I've ever worked with in the business.

Hulk *loved* Abyss – and he wanted to make the character as big as possible. Early into Hulk's tenure at TNA, there was a scene whereby Hulk gave his WWE Hall of Fame ring to Abyss. I know that people might scrunch up their face when they recall that segment, but it underscored the fact that Hulk was really quite committed to the Abyss character.

While I wasn't personally a fan of that character – it was a poor man's imitation of Mick Foley, in my book – Chris later made an unbelievable transition to an entirely different persona. After we wrote off Abyss from television for a while, Chris re-emerged as 'Joseph Park' – the supposed *brother* of Abyss – who also happened to be a practicing attorney! In his new role, Chris performed *far* beyond anybody's expectations, and to this day, it was some of the best character work that I've ever been involved in.

Eventually, 'Joseph' made his in-ring debut against Bully Ray – the former Bubba Ray Dudley - who himself was undergoing a major character transition. Having previously worked with Bully in WWE, I knew that he and I had pretty good chemistry, but I developed great *respect* for him once we got to TNA.

You often hear the term *psychology* as it applies to professional wrestling, but what it really comes down to is two things: a) knowing your audience, and b) being able to predict the reactions of that audience. Bully was outstanding in both of those areas, and once he became part of the creative process (specifically contributing to meetings on 'TV days'), he presented his ideas with a fearless passion. The more I listened to him, the more I was impressed by what he had to say.

In the creative arena, Bully was particularly strong at challenging the ideas presented by other people. Anybody can listen to an idea and say, 'I hate it – that sucks,' but that's not a *challenge* – that's just being stupid. Unless someone has a way of making a bad idea better, that type of attitude is simply a waste of time. It's just being a contrarian for the sake of it – or more often, a transparent attempt to convince everyone that you're actually involved.

Conversely, Bully was *constructive* with respect to how he responded to those ideas. I loved his approach, and ultimately, we developed a very close creative relationship. It's not like we agreed on everything – we didn't agree on some things, as a matter of fact – but professionally, his stock went sky high with me.

At the time Bully was coming into his own – having split from Devon Dudley *en route* to becoming a singles competitor – I approached him with an idea for a storyline. At the time, *Sons of Anarchy* was one of the biggest hits on television, and although it was a fictional show, it gave enough glimpses behind the scenes of the culture surrounding motorcycle clubs that it had a lot of authenticity. I thought that we could have success with a faction of wrestlers presented in a similar vein.

On one hand, I was a little hesitant to move forward with the idea, primarily because I knew what the response would be from some quarters: *Oh, he's just trying to recreate the nWo.*

That wasn't true, at all – and if you really look at it, the storyline, its background and the timing of everything was very unique indeed.

Besides, the idea of a faction is nothing new. Factions work in wrestling for a number of reasons; including the fact that it can be a great launching pad for other angles. You can take people out of a faction and engage them with many other characters on the roster. The real question was whether or not we had the right *talent* to portray the gimmick of an outlaw motorcycle club, which we eventually dubbed *The Aces & Eights*.

The *Aces & Eights* storyline was perhaps the culmination of everything I learned in WCW, the 10 years of experience I had in producing non-wrestling television with Jason, and the knowledge that I gained throughout that entire process. I was able to approach the *Aces & Eights* story from a vastly different perspective – and using a much different strategy – than I would have years earlier.

The fact is: I kind of got lucky with the nWo. Now don't get me wrong – I made a lot of good decisions with that storyline. I was operating on instinct, as much as anything else, and a fairly good idea of what I was hoping to achieve. But I didn't understand the concept of developing an *arc* for a storyline at that time. Consequently, while the nWo and its presentation was undoubtedly revolutionary – no-one had ever seen a reality-based story playing out over many months (or years) before – it didn't end up in the way that any of us wanted it to.

By the time I had influence in TNA, I was now formatting shows in such a way that reflected the importance of our storylines. I would classify those stories as either an 'A', 'B', 'C' or 'D' story – so as to frame the level of attention each would receive – and everything else, quite frankly, was an asterisk.

The 'A' story, for example, would likely revolve around the main event of the next pay-per-view. *That* story needed to get the maximum amount of time possible in the two-hour show. The 'B' story would be allocated an amount of time that was perhaps 15 or 20 percent less, and so on and so forth it went. It gave us a methodical method of taking a D-level storyline, in some cases, and *slowly* putting more of a focus on it – potentially, until it became a B or A-level story in its own right.

A strong rationale supporting this approach related to our relationship with Spike. As opposed to risking the appearance that we were just throwing shit against the wall every Thursday night, we now cultivated the perception that there was actually a *plan* – because there was one! To that end, I put together various three-month 'arcs' for Spike's examination and approval.

An additional benefit concerned the ability of our production staff to plan ahead, too. In the wrestling business, it's fairly typical for things to get done in the following way: *Yeah, I know it's late, and I didn't mean to wake you, but we need a video cut by tomorrow.* There are some places that can turn things around like that – WWE is brilliant at it – but it's not ideal by any stretch of the imagination.

Alternatively, if you give someone like Kevin Sullivan - the Head of post-production at TNA (and not to be confused with his 'Taskmaster' namesake) – a period of two months to prepare for an idea, it's going to end up as creative as it can possibly be. Kevin was a super creative guy, and he benefited from being able to look at our *story bible,* i.e. the document that contained pertinent details related to story and character development, in order to better do his job.

We were starting to make it a habit of thinking *long-term* about our creative process. If someone pitched me a great idea for an angle, I would listen to them and say, 'Okay – that's *week one.* What's week two? What's week three? How long does the storyline go on for? Let's back up from the end, work backwards and see how we can build the tension.'

Without that kind of planning, storylines can often fall flat. We see this quite often in wrestling today – there's a great angle that might kick off a storyline, but very little thought goes into how to follow it up. My experience has been that if you don't have some kind of framework – or an outline, even in bullet point form – you're just throwing shit against the wall and hoping it sticks.

The *Aces & Eights* saga is one of the storylines that I'm actually most proud of in my career. It was deliberate, very well considered and almost micromanaged in terms of the emotion that we created.

From the start, we had a solid idea of where we wanted to go – and who we wanted to feature. We knew that Bully was eventually going

116

to be revealed as the leader of the group, but to keep the suspense alive, we incorporated a number of other 'reveals' along the way.

Interestingly enough, Bully eventually became involved in a relationship with Brooke Hogan – Hulk's daughter – as part of the storyline. That development provided the catalyst for us to involve Hulk in the story, too, and at the end, Bully *turned* on Brooke – revealing that he had only dated her to get one over on Hulk Hogan.

I couldn't wait for the moment that we revealed Bully as the leader of *The Aces & Eights* (it eventually went down 10 months after the storyline began). When the moment finally came, the crowd response drew comparisons to Hulk's famous turn at *Bash at the Beach* – the ring was filled up with trash and debris.

For the record, that reaction was *organic*. It's what happens when you actually create *heat* – as opposed to the Pavlovian heat that we've all become accustomed to.

It was probably no coincidence that many of the people with whom I enjoyed working with in TNA featured in the culmination of my feud with Garett, at *Lockdown 2012* in Nashville, Tennessee.

As part of a 5-on-5, *Lethal Lockdown* cage match, 'Team Garett' (AJ Styles, Austin Aries, Mr. Anderson, Rob Van Dam and Garett) defeated 'Team Bischoff' (Bully Ray, Christopher Daniels, Gunner, Kazarian and myself) in comprehensive fashion, with Garett smashing a guitar over my head to get the pin!

I distinctly remember two things about the match. First and foremost, Loree was so disturbed by what she saw that she couldn't stomach watching it (in fairness, Garett ended up with some gnarly welts on his back). I had *tremendous* heat with 'Mrs. B' – as well as the 3,000 fans at the Nashville Municipal Auditorium – for the role that I played in that!

But secondly, I remember what happened after we got backstage. I looked at Garett and handed him something that was very important to me – a Rolex watch that Harvey Schiller, the former President of Turner Sports, gifted to me after WCW first turned a profit.

Here you are, kid, I said to Garett.

It's yours now.

While creatively, 2012 ended up being a very fulfilling year in TNA, the internal company chaos still reigned supreme. One of my consistent frustrations that year - with Dixie particularly - was TNA's continued reliance on big names. In my view, TNA was relying *exclusively* on its high equity talent – Hulk Hogan, Ric Flair, Kurt Angle and so on – as if to camouflage the fact that it wasn't making a commitment to improve the product otherwise.

Critics pointed to the fact that *Impact's* ratings were down for the year – falling from a 1.17 average in 2011 to a 1.01 average in 2012 – but that had nothing to do with our creative strategy.

To be crystal clear: TNA Wrestling being produced in a soundstage environment - regardless of what talent was on the card – was always going to hinder its growth.

The audience just got tired of it.

118

Look, we could have dropped The Undertaker into the center of the ring from a helicopter, and it would have been a big deal – for about two weeks. The minute that the audience witnessed The Undertaker, or John Cena, or The Rock – you name it – appearing in that environment, it would all have become meaningless. There would have been no difference on ratings, pay-per-view buy rates or any other metric.

Wrestling *needs* emotion from the audience to work – and it doesn't happen inside of a soundstage. The TNA product looked and sounded *small*, coming across mostly as a pale comparison to WWE.

While to her credit, Dixie wanted to be *competitive* with WWE, nobody wanted to make the financial commitment that was needed. Competing with WWE required money. It required a long-term strategy. It required *taking the show on the road* – and shooting it from legitimate venues.

In early 2013, Spike agreed to partially support an initiative to take TNA away from the *Impact Zone*, offsetting some of the increased production costs associated with the move. At the time, TNA's decision to leave the soundstage was advertised publicly as a "permanent" decision. "This is a tremendous step forward for TNA," stated Dixie. "Fans from around the world have been coming to us at Universal for more than eight years to be a part of the 'Impact Wrestling' audience. It's now time for us to take the 'Impact Wrestling' television cameras to them. This is a very important next evolution for the company."

Once *Impact* emanated from legitimate arenas, the difference in the show was striking. There was more energy. There was more excitement. There was more enthusiasm surrounding TNA as a property. But while it had been a great decision to get away from Universal, there wasn't an immediate, commensurate increase in ratings for the touring shows (that fact isn't surprising, by the way – it was unrealistic to expect a difference so quickly).

Therefore, within a matter of months, the touring strategy was abandoned – and TNA went back to the soundstage.

I mean, come on. Go back and watch some of those *Impact* shows. You'll see the same 25 people at ringside – each and every show - for three fucking years!

By that time, people had been conditioned to watching WWE – and earlier, WCW – broadcasting in front of 10, 20, 30, 40 or 50 thousand people. The standard was set for what a wrestling show *needed to look like* – at least to be considered a viable, legitimate television product.

You can't reach that goal in a fucking soundstage – you just can't.

GRATEFUL

Behind this beautiful smile was a woman, sometimes overwhelmed by raising 3 young kids and caring for a handicapped husband, but determined to make her family's life as happy as possible.

Visiting my childhood home in Roseville.

My father, Kenneth Bischoff.

Me and Loree - 38 years and still going strong.

From left: Loree, myself, Garett, Mary Jane, Waylon James and
Montanna. This is what 'Grateful' looks like!

Stevie was a great companion.   Nickie takes in another beautiful
morning.

Giddy up...it's Waylon James Bischoff, the newest member of our
family. You can call him 'WayJay'!

Garett during his tenure with
TNA, circa 2013.

Loree and I congratulate
Montanna after her 4th
marathon(!).

Walking Amanda down
the aisle.

126

On July 31st, 2022, I was privileged to witness Ric Flair's Last Match in Nashville.

'83 Weeks' proved to be so successful that we took the show on the road.

Enjoying a Charity Softball game with some old WCW friends: Ernest Miller, Sonny Onoo and Jim Duggan.

Sent Home

11

As it turned out, 2013 is when the wheels *really* started falling off for TNA. The biggest issue, among many other things, was simple: *cash flow*.

At the time, Bruce Prichard was handling talent relations (having first been brought in to replace Vince Russo as Head Writer), effectively operating as a liaison between talent and the Carter family – while much of the roster wasn't getting paid on time. As a result, Bruce found himself as the consummate 'fall guy' of sorts, catching flak from wrestlers who were fed - upon contacting the office when their checks failed to show up – a never-ending trail of bullshit.

Yeah, the check is in the mail…

…It was Fed-Exed a week ago, so it must be a problem with Fed-Ex…

…Actually, the check was returned. Did you change your address?

The talent was hearing every excuse that you could possibly think of, and clearly, this became a very problematic situation. Hulk made his final TNA appearance in October, and soon after, many other high-profile names moved on from the company. It was reported that TNA was 'offering' talent as much as a 60% pay cut to stay on.

It was obvious that major changes were afoot, especially once Dixie hired John 'Big' Gaburick – a producer who had just been let go by WWE – as TNA's Executive Vice President of Television Production.

Somehow, John had convinced Dixie that he was previously the 'right-hand man' to Kevin Dunn – the long-time Executive Producer of WWE programming – and that was all she needed to hear. As such, John became the latest bright, shiny object from WWE that was *certain* to make a huge contribution to TNA. "He is a gifted and innovative storyteller," said Dixie of John in a company press release. "We are thrilled to have him on board."

In fairness, John *is* a fantastic producer. As a talent in WWE, I got along with him great, and found him to be very smart; very talented. He was often a lot of fun to be around, but I was never sure what he did before he started working for Kevin Dunn. I was told that John was either a UPS driver or worked for UPS in some capacity – at least until Kevin took John under his wing, mentored him and taught him production from the ground up.

Initially, it was John, Bruce and myself working together – and everything was just fine. While TNA already had some talented producers – Kevin Sullivan, for example, who created some magnificent promo videos, and David Sahadi, who had also worked with WWE in the past – I thought that adding John would only help move us forward.

My optimism didn't last long.

Ultimately, the relationship between John and I became tense. He was trying to dip his toes into waters that he didn't have anything to do with – creative matters especially. That's always going to end up badly – and it did.

Evidently, John was positioning himself to take as much control over TNA as he could. He wanted to be the guy 'calling the shots' – and quite honestly, I understood that. I wasn't too concerned about it; after all, I had a contract – a very specific agreement, as noted, detailing my role in TNA, and specifically, what I would (and wouldn't) do.

Nonetheless, the tension kept building.

Dixie never liked confrontation of *any* kind, which is not a great quality for someone running a wrestling company. She was *conflict-averse* at the best of times, and with that in mind, I knew that if further changes were coming, she would not be the person delivering the news.

It was via Jason Hervey - who himself enjoyed more of a social relationship with Dixie – that I learned what was coming next. *Eric, he advised, here's what Dixie wants you to do moving forward.*

A TNA attorney followed up with the edict in writing, detailing that my new role, apparently, was to watch the show, make notes, and provide my input – without ever being present at the actual tapings.

As I had already taken myself off television (Garett gave my character his comeuppance, in a segment that aired in April 2012, in the conclusion to our storyline), I didn't care about *that* possibility - returning as an on-screen character - being rendered impossible. I didn't need the money, either, but at the same time, I wasn't going to look around at TNA's situation – with everything being on fire around me – and say, 'Okay – here's the fire exit!'

131

Simply *collecting a check* was never something I was interested in, so I took their little letter, read over it, and said to myself, 'Okay, I'll watch the show, make notes and give them my input.'

They didn't listen to any of my input – that part is obvious – but I did what was stated on the letter. *Every single week.*

In an effort to quell the growing discord among TNA's talent – the checks were now bouncing faster than the lies could be generated – the company called a meeting to discuss the issue. Presiding over the summit was an attorney representing TNA – someone who I will refrain from mentioning by name – but an absolute dweeb who oversaw legal issues related to the company.

This attorney was one of those people who really wishes he was 6-foot-4 and 300 pounds – or someone who could physically intimidate people. He had one of the biggest Napoleon complexes that I've ever seen. He was just this little worm who nobody – not least of which a roster of professional wrestlers – would even dream of taking seriously.

The lady who ran catering could have kicked his ass.

Anyway, this little jackass came out – at the very outset of the meeting – and really tried to intimidate everyone in attendance (many of whom, as stated, were still not getting paid!). He actually attempted to issue a threat to the assembled talent, informing the group that he was *such* a great lawyer – a legend in his own mind, apparently – that he would end up costing them *more* money if they didn't play by TNA's rules.

Off to the side – along with a couple of other people in management - I sat and listened to this *drek* in amazement (typically, I would rather be anywhere else but a TNA meeting, but my curiosity got the better of me this time). I looked around the room and saw Garett sitting along with the rest of the talent. As the jackass attorney droned on – puffing out his chest in an effort to appear taller than 3-foot-5 – Garett and I caught eyes at the exact same time.

From across the room, we basically said the same thing to each other.

Are you fucking kidding me with this?

For a while in 2014, I continued to make my producer notes from home (admittedly, the tone of my feedback oscillated with the stupidity of TNA's programming) – as I had been instructed - until TNA simply quit paying me.

To this day, the company (or whatever the hell is left of it, as trying to follow the saga of what happened to TNA, throughout its various incarnations, tends to make my head hurt) owes me about $90,000 (incidentally, they owe Garett about $15,000, too).

They just stopped paying.

I'm not a big fan of litigation, but in this case, I started legal proceedings in an attempt to recoup some of those funds. Eventually, as the bills started to mount up, I was advised that the legal costs associated with pursuing TNA were likely to far exceed the money I was owed.

I resigned myself to saying, 'You know what? Fuck it. Just move on. They are what they are, and they did what they did. You went into this knowing it was kind of a sketchy situation. That's on you – just let it go.'

I advised the same thing to Garett, too: *just let it go.*

Garett soon made the choice – in a wise decision, although I would have supported him either way – to move on entirely from the wrestling business.

In July 2014, reports circulated that Spike had finally tired of TNA, too – putting themselves in the company of a great number of performers who felt the exact same way. *Impact Wrestling* was dropped from the network by year's end, only accelerating the death spiral that TNA found itself involved in (I sometimes wondered if it was an intentional death spiral, by virtue of how the talent – and sometimes management – was treated).

From a purely business perspective, TNA made a habit of engaging in things that were just suicidal. By the end of my association with the company, *everybody* was being lied to – seemingly on a weekly basis - and due to the volume of bounced checks, I was hearing stories of wrestlers getting their cars repossessed, or being unable to feed their families. The shit that Bruce had to deal with was just *ridiculous* – another book could be written on that subject alone.

While I had previous experience in dealing with a dysfunctional corporate environment – *see: TBS, Inc., circa 1998-99* – this was at a much more amateur level. It was extremely disappointing, in part because inevitably – as a result of the well-documented WCW story, the mythology of the *Monday Night Wars*, and the pre-existing profile that I had in the wrestling business – there existed a perception that everything 'wrong' with TNA was due to Eric Bischoff and Hulk Hogan.

In truth, neither Hulk or I had *anything* to do with TNA's budgets, hiring, firing, operations, promotion, or really anything that related to their business model. My involvement – which admittedly escalated over time - was limited to *creative*, and while I had a loud, perhaps obnoxious voice in that arena (Dixie always made the final creative decisions, by the way), that was really the extent of it.

For the record, I regard some of that creative – the *Aces and Eights* saga, most notably – as some of the best storytelling that I've ever had a hand in. On a creative level, I also got to work directly with my son, and there's not one memory that I have – going all the way back to when I started with the AWA to present day – that is more valuable to me than that.

In a healthy, positive, constructive way, I was able to provide Garett with an opportunity to fulfill his dream – and to be able to participate in that dream with him. And make no mistake about it, it *was* his dream – to work with his father, on a nationally televised wrestling show, together on camera. In doing so, he went through a host of difficulties to gain the respect of the locker room, and ultimately, he overcame all of those inherent challenges that arose when we discussed the idea initially.

Nothing comes close to the value that I put on that shared experience with Garett – and he will remember that for the rest of his life.

I'll always be grateful to Dixie Carter and TNA for making that possible.

As for Dixie: in the final analysis, she was never the person calling the shots – her *parents* called the shots. She was caught in the middle as much as I was, and in her own way – elegant and professional, as always – Dixie tried to do the best job she could. While she had responsibility over some important lower-level matters (hiring talent, for example), the *real* management of TNA (including the development of a *vision* for the company) was never within her purview.

The real issue was simple: *there was a complete lack of vision for the company*. There wasn't a five-year plan, or even a three-year plan – hell, there wasn't even a one-year plan! That wasn't entirely Dixie's fault, by the way, but ultimately, it made me just throw up my hands in resignation.

Fuck it.

Even today, it's difficult for me to talk about TNA – mostly because it was such a missed opportunity. The *coup de gras* - and something that I remain livid about – occurred when its management, figuratively of course, decided to pick up a shotgun, shoot themselves in both feet, and then shoot themselves in the head.

Specifically, there was an opportunity presented to TNA's ownership on a *silver platter*. It happened when UFC left Spike (and its parent company, Viacom) in favor of the Fox network, a decision that caused Kevin Kay, the President of Spike, to facilitate Viacom's purchase of Bellator – the second largest MMA promotion. Kevin's rationale - which made complete sense to me, incidentally - was to avoid a future scenario whereby Spike promoted content that could eventually air elsewhere. Moving forward, it was decided that if Spike were going to build a business (as had been the case with UFC), they wanted to own at least a piece of that business.

136

After I became aware of this, I *personally* pushed for Viacom to buy an equity stake in TNA. If TNA was *owned* by its television network, I thought, the likelihood of its continued viability increased exponentially – surely, that part was obvious.

Kevin was interested, as were a number of other Viacom executives.

Guess who wasn't interested?

Management.

I found myself asking a familiar question.

Are you fucking kidding me?

Rather than having a television network as a business partner – thus ensuring TNA's longevity as a franchise – the decision was made to reject the proposal instead. As a result, it became clear that someday – supposing that Spike canceled *Impact Wrestling*, as eventually did happen – TNA would have to shop its content to other networks, essentially starting over from scratch.

Well, good luck with that, I thought to myself, chuckling at the idea of TV executives *grappling* with the prospect – pun intended - of putting *TNA Wrestling* on their airwaves (*sans* Hulk Hogan, Sting, Kurt Angle, AJ Styles, Rob Van Dam, and, to a lesser extent, Eric Bischoff).

It all just makes my brain explode.

Shit Hits The Fan

12

It took a long time for me to get comfortable with – and even to wrap my head around - the idea of doing personal appearances. I can't really say why, exactly; I just knew that whenever I would get offers to do appearances, I would always turn them down.

By virtue of the success that Jason and I had experienced with BHE, there was never much time to entertain such events anyway. I was busy; plus, I really didn't need the money, quite honestly. I felt that my time was at a premium.

There was also another reason why the idea of signing autographs at a convention, or doing a personal appearance of that nature didn't appeal to me. It was probably a result of my ego, or maybe just good old-fashioned pride – if there's any difference between the two. It was just an *uncomfortable* notion for me. I knew that I didn't look like the Eric Bischoff that was pictured on the 8x10's that I was signing. That might be hard for some readers to relate to, but at the time, that's how I felt.

But then, as 2014 rolled around, *shit really hit the fan*. While Jason and I had enjoyed a lot of success with BHE since its formation in 2003, things in television were really starting to change. We realized that while we had been big enough to be successful – we had created and produced reality television for almost every cable outlet – we had never been big enough to be *acquired* (or, alternatively, to have the opportunity to work exclusively with a major studio).

139

That fact mattered as the television industry shifted. It had become much more competitive within the marketplace (and across the entertainment landscape more generally); consequently, cable outlets and networks were now very cautious about trying new shows, new concepts – anything *new*. What had been, with respect to 'non-scripted' or reality television specifically, kind of like a wild, wild, west environment previously – we had literally pitched shows on the back of a bar napkin – now resembled a process that was both more difficult and time consuming.

Moreover, the profit margins were beginning to get *crushed*. Producing television shows became much less of a profitable venture, and due to the increased competition, there was less and less volume for an independent production company like ours. The pressure seriously started to mount on Jason and I, and eventually, we came to an important realization. Quite simply, times had changed – *we* had changed – everything had changed, really. We didn't see ourselves competing at the level that was needed to be financially successful, and therefore, we agreed to dissolve BHE.

In addition to Jason and I going our separate ways, my involvement with TNA had come to an end, too. Now believe me, while there were no tears shed - or a minute of emotion about no longer being a part of TNA – the combination of losing both sources of income meant an abrupt halt in cash flow.

I had been living pretty well over the previous 20 years, making significant amounts of money along the way. Nonetheless, I wasn't nearly where I would've *liked* to have been when BHE (and, to a lesser extent, TNA) came to an end. Then again, for a long time, everything had been going my way.

For that reason, it was a surprise to many when it came out – quite a long time after the fact, incidentally – that I eventually had to file for Chapter 11 bankruptcy.

It was embarrassing - firstly, being at the stage of my life when most people are looking at their 401ks growing and growing, or maybe their houses have just been paid off, things like that.

But here I was – essentially starting over, at 62 years old.

A lot of things precipitated my filing for bankruptcy, despite having made millions and millions of dollars over my career. One of the biggest factors was that as an entrepreneur, I was always attracted to risk.

It's easy to see *potential* in an opportunity, but it's not so easy to understand how to manage the risk involved in it. Naturally, if I see an opportunity – and I'm convinced in that opportunity – I don't give a shit about the risk. I don't even wanna talk about it, other than, 'Ok, we'll write down the risk – or risks – on a piece of paper,' but that's about it. I was always so laser focused on the *opportunity* side of the equation.

As an entrepreneur, one of the characteristics that has always worked for me is having no fear. I have no fear of anything – or anyone – other than fearing for my family's health and safety. But when it comes to anything outside of my family, I just don't have any fear.

I'm not afraid to fail, as is often the case with people who have been entrepreneurs throughout their lives. I always believed that no challenge was too big, that there was always a solution to whatever problems I - or my business partners – may have encountered. I would look at something that was working and say, 'Wow – there's a great opportunity there. What if *I* do that?'

Loree was always the logical one: *Well, how are you going to do that?*

My response was always the same: *I'll figure it out.*

I didn't necessarily figure things out all by myself, by the way. I would 'tag in' people who possessed more experience than I did in certain areas. Nonetheless, *the answers are out there*, I always thought.

Inherently, people are often afraid – even more so now, because it's so easy for others to judge you, with social media and everything else in our culture. But as an entrepreneur, if I operate from a position of fear – if I think, 'Yeah, what if it *doesn't* work…what if I can't raise the money…what if I can't figure it out…' – I'm toast.

At the same time, once I had to file for Chapter 11, I realized that I needed to get a little smarter with respect to managing risk.

One of the reasons that I ended up in the bankruptcy situation was that my wife and I saw a great opportunity – there's that word again – which resulted in the *Buffalo Bill Cody Beer* project. That became a really interesting…education, shall we say.

Both Loree and I observed that here in Cody, Wyoming, Buffalo Bill (full name William Frederick Cody) - is all over everything, from the hotel that he built in downtown Cody, to the historical society in town which happens to be one of the biggest Western history museums in the world. Every year, two million people drive through Cody, Wyoming, on their way to Yellowstone.

One night in 2009, Loree and I said to each other, 'Wait a minute. We've got two million people that drive through here – people from all over the world. They love Yellowstone, the Rocky Mountains, all that Western stuff...and in the summertime, every other storefront is a Western souvenir type of place. We should come up with a *Buffalo Bill Cody* beer, offer it for sale here in town, and make sure that everybody that drives home leaves with a six-pack of our beer – to go along with their hat, a t-shirt and a bumper sticker.'

That was the idea.

During the peak tourist season, the people that do business in Cody make a *fortune*. They open up their souvenir shops in May, close them down in October, and seemingly go to Hawaii for the rest of the year. Well, fast forward a couple of years after our little brainstorming exercise, and I had *invested* a fortune towards making the idea a reality – about a quarter million dollars of my *own* money.

Retirement savings – fuck that. Who needs to retire? Cash that 401k if we need to!

To be clear, it didn't start out as a quarter million-dollar investment. It started out with the trademark process – exploring and applying for a trademark, pretty simple stuff. At the time, my attorney said, 'Ah – this'll only cost 10 or 15 thousand dollars. We'll get the Buffalo Bill Cody trademark locked up – there's no other competing trademarks out there.'

Sure, I thought, *sounds great – I can do that.*

Once we actually got involved in the process – as legal things often go – it became more complex. The next conversation we had was more along the lines of, 'Well, Eric…here's some of the *challenges* we're having. It's gonna take a little more time.'

Ok, I said, *how much more money is it gonna cost?*

Five or ten grand, was the reply. *Five or ten grand - tops.*

So now I'm in about 20 or 25 thousand dollars.

Soon it was 45 or 50 thousand dollars.

That process was to continue for a period of two years.

What started out as a cute little vanity project was turning into an exhaustive – not to mention serious – legal battle over the trademark. The August 27th, 2011 edition of *The Wall Street Journal* even picked up on the story:

Two Businessmen Launch New Brews Named After Wild West Legend; Feud Coming to a Head

CODY, Wyo.—The Wild West legend who founded this town is widely honored—and marketed—here.

…Yet there has never been a Buffalo Bill beer here—until now.

This summer, two local businessmen each launched a brew named after their hometown hero. Now it looks like the town isn't big enough for both.

The two entrepreneurs are fighting in court for the exclusive right to sell beer that trades on the musky aura of adventure surrounding Army-scout-turned-bison-hunter-turned-sharpshooting-showman William F. Cody.

In one corner: Former professional wrestling icon Eric Bischoff.

…Yearning to diversify, Mr. Bischoff hired a microbrewery to create a light, spicy rye that he is marketing as Buffalo Bill Cody Beer, "the spirit of the wild wild West."

His chief rival: Mike Darby, whose family owns and operates Buffalo Bill's Irma Hotel, a historic landmark built by Buffalo Bill in 1902 and decorated with truly enormous big-game trophies. The hotel has been selling drinks in Buffalo Bill glasses from Buffalo Bill's Bar for years, until it finally occurred to Mr. Darby, he says, that he needed a branded beverage to carry the theme to its logical end.

…The fight between Mr. Bischoff and Mr. Darby has grown increasingly nasty. Legal claims and counterclaims are piling high, and neither man is giving an inch.

"There's only one Buffalo Bill, so there's only one Buffalo Bill Beer," Mr. Darby says.

"Just because I don't like to fight doesn't mean I'm not good at it," says Mr. Bischoff.

A state judge who tried to sort out the dispute at a hearing in July threw up his hands in frustration. Mr. Darby, he noted, got his beer to market first, by two days.

But Mr. Darby failed to get federal approval of his label, as required by the law. (Mr. Darby says he thought the brewer and distributor had taken care of that.)

Mr. Bischoff did get his label approved, and also applied for a federal trademark. Mr. Darby didn't—yet he insists that his hotel's long association with Buffalo Bill makes him the rightful owner of the brand.

I had hit the quarter-million-dollar mark by the time the article came out – and that was just in legal fees. That figure doesn't include the startup costs, and all of the things associated with actually producing and distributing a beer. I had distribution in Wyoming, Colorado,

Nevada, and Arizona, but due to the ongoing trademark dispute, it was becoming an extremely expensive vanity project.

For obvious reasons, the project was no longer fun anymore – for reasons that I couldn't have anticipated at the start. Now, in order to continue, I was going to have to seriously scale up the operation, as both the profit margins associated with selling beer and the heavy regulatory issues meant that a one-brand company was extremely impractical – just to begin with!

There's just no way that you can come out with one brand of beer, distribute it, and expect to have success. I didn't know that going in, but at the same time, it wasn't my *goal* to run a grand operation at the beginning. My goal was to sell that six-pack of beer alongside that hat, t-shirt and bumper sticker.

Ultimately, I learned *a lot* about the beer business. I could sit down and teach a class about the 'business of the beer business', you might say. It's a whole lot different than most people think.

It turned out to be a *sobering* experience for my wife and I (see what I did there?). It cost us a ton of cash, and ultimately – although we still own the trademark – we decided to fold up shop.

Around the same time as the abandoned beer project, I became heavily involved in the online gaming industry. While at the time, gambling in the U.S. was fairly limited to Las Vegas, Atlantic City, or Indian Casinos, among other places, Europe was an entirely different environment. All over the continent, you could come into storefronts to buy lottery tickets, play slot machines and indulge in other things to that effect.

146

Therefore, I got involved in celebrity branded digital slot machines, whereby players throughout Europe – and certain parts of the world, where it was legal – would play online games such as *Hulk Hogan's Hulkamania* (think leg drops instead of bells and cherries) and *The Hoff* featuring David Hasselhoff. We ended up licensing games with Dennis Rodman, Chuck Norris, Joe Frazier and the Blues Brothers as well. It was a *highly* lucrative business at the outset.

In the end, however, that particular venture – *MX Digital* – cost all of us combined (I wasn't the only investor) an even *bigger* fortune (think: seven figures). While we had done all of our homework, completed all of the necessary due diligence, and partnered with the right people to make the idea successful, it ultimately didn't work. We had entered a highly regulated business and seemingly overnight, the regulations in Europe all changed.

I had now depleted all of my resources - including my retirement savings and everything else – because I really believed in both the *Buffalo Bill Cody* and *MX Digital* projects. Everybody involved saw the same vision, but each of those investments didn't work out - for a variety of reasons that couldn't really have been predicted.

According to the bankruptcy plan, I had six years to pay off the debts that we had incurred (often called the *reorganization* chapter, Chapter 11 bankruptcy allows for the restructuring of existing debt. Every single dollar would need to be repaid). Loree and I had substantial debt. That is: substantial IRS debt. Substantial business debt. Substantial personal debt. It all had to be taken care of at the same time. The news hit us hard, and we had to downsize – fast.

We had multiple homes that needed to be taken care of. At the same time, I now had to figure out what to do with the rest of my life. Having to file for bankruptcy was hard on my ego. *I've made millions of dollars*, I thought to myself. *Why the hell am I in this position?*

I knew the answer, ultimately: it was because I loved taking risks. It's in my nature. I did a lot of things that had I *not* done, it wouldn't have mattered if BHE and TNA went away.[1]

But that's not how I've ever lived my life. I've always been an entrepreneur. I've always enjoyed the thrill of the hunt. I've never

---

[1] The intervening period – between my departure from TNA and filing for bankruptcy - was notable for two long-form interviews that I was the subject of: firstly, my appearance on Stone Cold Steve Austin's popular podcast, and secondly, my guesting on *Legends with JBL*, an original show on the WWE Network. The latter appearance did much to suggest that WWE's portrayal of WCW - and the *Monday Nights Wars* more generally – was in the process of becoming fairer.

That notion was confirmed when WWE produced *Eric Bischoff: Sports Entertainment's Most Controversial Figure* in 2016. I found myself ending the documentary in philosophical fashion:

"The war - as people like to call it – between WWE and WCW...or me and Vince McMahon...or Vince McMahon and Ted Turner...however you wanna look at it...turned out exactly the way it should have turned out.

"And I'm glad that it turned out the way that it did. I'm glad that Vince McMahon and WWE came out on top - in that particular situation. I'm glad because had it been different – had WCW/Turner Broadcasting/AOL Time Warner/whoever ended up coming out on top...we wouldn't be sitting here right now.

"There would be no WWE Network. There would be so many things that are so important to so many millions of people around the world that wouldn't exist.

"...Turner/AOL Time Warner...Eric Bischoff, for that matter...wouldn't have had the commitment to the industry that Vince McMahon has.

"That's just a fact."

been afraid of taking a risk, and if I fail, I've always believed that I can come back.

I hoped that I could come back this time.

Soon enough, it became apparent that under such financial hardship, I needed to do some extra work on the weekends, so to speak. I certainly wouldn't be able to drive out to an indy show again for a *gratis* appearance – at least for a while – and so I started rethinking my stance on personal appearances. Eventually, I took one - more or less to see what it was like – to see if I would enjoy it.

Spoiler alert: *I didn't.*

Part of the reason was the travel; I *resented* having to get on a plane, especially on a weekend, because travel has become so much more difficult over the years. As I took a few more bookings - trying to stabilize things from a financial point of view - I found myself wanting to go home as soon as I arrived at the venue.

I want to be clear here – it was never about the fans. The fans were always great and, in large part, actually made my time away from home a little bit easier. I would occasionally have an interaction that would help me forget, albeit for a moment, the fact that I resented having to be there.

But at this stage of my life, I invariably came back to thinking, *why do I have to do this?*

Whether I liked it or not, the income, at that point, was extremely important. So I agonized through each and every appearance, kicking myself for putting myself in that position. It was just something I had to do – no longer was I asking myself, 'Do I want to do these appearances?'

No, in my mind, I *had* to do those appearances – and I struggled through them all.

A Failed Experiment

13

Now outside of the *day-to-day* wrestling business - ostensibly for good – I found myself looking closer at the overall scene. I noticed that beyond WWE, a burgeoning independent movement was starting to emerge, aided in particular by social media and the Internet more broadly. The technology had advanced to the point where independent companies could buy a couple cameras for 300 hundred dollars apiece, an inexpensive 'switcher' from Amazon, a lighting rig, and end up producing for themselves a fairly decent show. Consequently, I thought about hosting the content produced by these various 'indy' groups on a single platform online, aggregating the shows together and creating virtual 'territories' for each region. Then, perhaps once a year, the top two or three stars from each territory would get together for a big show hosted on my platform – *the 'Super Bowl' of Independent Wrestling.*

In essence, the concept would effectively see the merging of modern wrestling (its style, presentation and modes of production) with the territorial *structure* that had historically been very successful. I worked on the idea alone for about a year before bringing it to Nick Hausman, a contributor with *Wrestlezone*, one of the biggest news sites in the industry.

Subsequently, Nick and I began preparations to launch the *IRW Network,* detailed as such to fans in a breathless press release:

On the eve of WrestleMania 33, former WCW President and RAW General Manager Eric Bischoff is announcing his latest endeavor: *IRWNetwork.com*, officially launching on June 1st!

...*IRW* stands for *Indies Rule the World* and has been a project that Bischoff has been developing for over a year. The *IRW Network*'s mission is to give popular independent artists, wrestlers and entities the ability to launch their own over the top channels and offer fans premium content at a low price point of between $1.99-$3.99 per month.

...Here is what Bischoff had to say this past Thursday night in regards to the launch: "It will really be a hub for all things independent wrestling and culture. We are going to have thousands of hours of some of the best wrestling footage from around the world available. People will be able to log on, download and enjoy. We are going to have podcasts with some of the top podcasters from around the world. We are going to have all kinds of great content. Thousands and thousands of hours. Some of the best independent promotions from around the world. I am very excited [about it]."

...*IRWNetwork.com* also features a fan forum as well as a global calendar that will begin to be filled with details about independent events from around the world. An IRW app that will pair with the site will be rolled out as well before the official launch on June 1st.

In an effort to 'bridge the gap' between the announcement and the launch date, Nick and I produced a series of premium podcast episodes on the website, offered only to early subscribers of the service. We called them 'overrun' episodes, due to the fact that Nick and I were *already* producing a free weekly podcast – *Bischoff on Wrestling* – which had launched the previous summer.

Podcasting had been on my radar for some time, simply because I was hearing about it *constantly* – seemingly everyone in the wrestling industry was getting involved in it. Throughout 2015, I had flirted with the idea of going into *radio* – one of the biggest names in that industry tapped me to do a show for syndication – but ultimately, the deal didn't work out. In any event, podcasting, not radio, was clearly ascendant by the time *Bischoff on Wrestling* debuted.

Prior to meeting Nick, I had three or four other people reach out to me about the subject. In each case, I would start asking questions that I genuinely didn't know the answers to. I wanted to find out if they knew more about the podcasting business than I did, and in particular, if they had any idea about what the business model might be. The answers I received were always pretty vague, and I could tell that they didn't have much of an idea about how to attract advertisers. In fact, they didn't have much of an idea about *anything* – other than an awareness that wrestling podcasters were apparently getting paid and that they wanted to jump in. Needless to say, I turned all of those opportunities down.

To be completely honest, when Nick approached me about *Bischoff on Wrestling*, I didn't walk away with the feeling that he had a real strong grasp on how - from a financial perspective - to make it work either. Nonetheless, I was impressed with Nick's enthusiasm - his sheer energy – and I believe I even said, albeit at the time, that he reminded me of myself at a younger age. I also saw some value in his relationship with *Wrestlezone*, as far as its potential to give us some kind of platform – and some means of building an immediate audience. But once we actually got started with the show (*Bischoff on Wrestling* premiered on July 27th, 2016), it became clear that there was no real format to our show, and no identity around it – other than my name being attached to it.

As a first effort, *Bischoff on Wrestling* did *okay*. We had some listeners – it wasn't *embarrassing* or anything – but it certainly wasn't generating any kind of revenue. And I wasn't looking for another hobby – especially one that increasingly became a chore to complete.

After a while, as listeners could probably tell for themselves, the chemistry between Nick and I really started to wear down. Nick is a very extreme liberal – a textbook 'woke' kind of evangelist – whose preaching tends to lack any knowledge, understanding of history, or life experience. In general, that situation is fine with me – I have a lot of friends on the opposite end of the political spectrum – and I don't judge people by their politics (only their *character*, and quite frankly, how much fun they are to be around).

The problem became that Nick wanted to have these grand political debates as part of our show. He thought it would be great to have these opposing voices discussing various 'hot button' political issues, which was more or less easy for me – I'm a fairly opinionated person to begin with. But as we got into it, the facts were clearly not on Nick's side. He usually had a lot of emotion to support his points - but very little in the way of facts.

That works fine if you're making passing comments on something, or if you're just parroting something that appeals to your sense of identity, but when you get into an actual discussion about a topic – and particularly when only one person can reflect on historical parallels, or what works and doesn't work – all of a sudden, the wheels fall off. In my experience, highly emotional people tend to get *more* emotional in that situation, and Nick ended up in that place a lot.

It got to the point where after one episode, I thought to myself, 'This is just stupid. We're not making any money. There's no prospect of making any money. This kid is just exploring his *wokism* and he obviously wants to be in the wrestling business.'

I felt that Nick was using his relationship with me to try and raise his profile within the industry. He desperately wanted to be a wrestling announcer, or a host of a wrestling show, and I think he believed our association would help him towards that end. It became obvious to me what was going on.

154

I finally called Nick one day and said, 'Let's take a break. Let's go on hiatus and then after the first of the year, let's reconvene, and see if this is something we still want to do.'

In fairness, I think by that time, Nick was real tired of *me*, too – and he was probably just as relieved as I was. But for all the 'hiatus' talk, I made up my mind within a week – *that was that*.

Bischoff on Wrestling (and, before it ever really started, the *IRW Network* idea) was done.

As it turned out, *Bischoff on Wrestling* wasn't a complete write-off. There *were* a couple of good things that came out of that experiment – including, most memorably, a two-part interview that we aired with Lex Luger.

For the longest time, it was no secret that I wasn't the biggest fan of Lex – real name Larry Pfohl – for a couple of reasons in particular. Firstly, it had been my experience that Lex, at least during the time that we worked together in WCW, was an obnoxiously arrogant person. When in 1993, the WWF introduced Luger in the character of 'The Narcissist', well... I didn't think it was a stretch.

While famously, Lex made a huge impact with a surprise appearance on the debut edition of *Nitro* – while subsequently enjoying a great run as a babyface – I wasn't tripping over myself to bring him in. With full knowledge of his backstage reputation, I low-balled an offer of $150,000 per year (far less than Lex was making with the WWF), not thinking twice if my offer got refused. To Lex's credit, he accepted the deal, eventually proved himself, and parlayed his initial situation into a much more lucrative contract.

Nonetheless, my dislike of Lex continued – and soon intensified greatly. On May 1st, 2003, Elizabeth Hulette – better known in the wrestling industry as Miss Elizabeth – died in the home they shared together. The cause of her death was listed as 'acute toxicity' - specifically induced by a mix of painkillers and vodka – and I held Lex responsible. As far as I was concerned, he had influenced Liz and ultimately led her down that tragic path.

I was devastated that Liz was gone.

Several years later, Lex suffered a nerve impingement in his neck, ending up in a quadriplegic state for a period of time. The damage was attributed to an accumulation of disc injuries, bone spurs and other spinal trauma he had collected as a wrestler and football player. As time went on, he would require the use of a wheelchair on a regular basis – something he relies on fully at the time of this writing.

Shortly after his injury, I had heard that Lex had apparently developed a new attitude. His mindset was captured in an *Atlanta Journal-Constitution* piece of the time:

"I was one of the strongest guys on the planet," Luger said recently. "I was freaky strong before. I was bench-pressing 450 pounds my senior year of high school. I was a freak. Now I can't lift a one-pound dumbbell.

"But God tells me that mind, body and spirit and what we are as a man is measured not by our physical strength, but our inner strength."

Luger, whose real name is Lawrence Pfohl, now takes great pride in each day's small victories. Things like getting showered and shaved on his own in only 30 minutes or standing a little bit more each day. Things like trying to gradually make full amends with estranged family members he took for granted over the years, including his 17- and 21-year-old children.

The new and humbled Lex Luger is a man of strong religious conviction whose faith has helped him remain mostly upbeat.

Luger has taken it upon himself to minister to young patients at the Shepherd Center, often telling them his story of widespread abuse of drugs, steroids and alcohol at the expense of his family and health.

Luger believes he was meant to lift their spirits and give personal testimony to the importance of doing things the right way.

Over time, my feelings towards Lex softened. I would read some of the things he would post on social media, for example, and it made me think, 'Hmmm. Maybe he *has* turned his life around.' Obviously, Lex had gone through some *major* challenges, and although I wasn't *fully* convinced of his transformation, I didn't have the same level of animosity or resentment towards him.

On a few occasions, I bumped into Lex at some personal appearances, but I wasn't sure about his thoughts on an in-depth interview. I didn't know how open he would be towards being transparent in that kind of a format. But to my surprise, when I reached out to him about it, he was more than anxious to take part.

It became one of the most amazing interviews that I ever did.

Stunningly, Lex opened up at a level that I couldn't have anticipated:

I'll never forget the early morning hours when Liz passed away. We were just watching movies together - sipping on some vodka and popping pills…

…I realized that she had stopped breathing, Eric. Five minutes before that, she was standing at the microwave and I was heating up some food…and she literally got up and stood right next to me and wanted help. I told her to sit down and that I 'had it'…[so] she sat down and I went back to fixing what was mine.

I look back now at the fragility, the recklessness and the carelessness…we didn't know that we were playing Russian Roulette. Some of the guys, Eric - most of the guys - had a wife and kids. They wanted to wake up the next morning. [But] just the danger - playing with the drugs like that. One minute she was there - and the next minute I was wondering why she wasn't eating and trying to wake her up. I realized she wasn't breathing, [so I'm] panicking and calling 911.

The tragedy of that. To witness that first hand...I'll never forget.

By the end of the conversation, both Lex and I were near tears. I decided to open up myself with some final comments:

I need to be really honest with you, at this point...

There was a long time - after Elizabeth passed - that I held a grudge. While I wasn't close to Elizabeth, my wife was - and [with me] not knowing...not understanding...not being there...not living in your shoes...it was easy for me to judge.

It was hard for me to think that your life had turned around – *really*. Too often, people use faith as a crutch – or use it as camouflage – and they don't *really* believe. They don't really 'walk the walk' – they just 'talk it'...to help them get through the moment. But I have to say, at this point, there are tears in my eyes...and I am so proud of you.

I respect you so much for what you've become, who you are, and the amount of influence that you can have on people.

By the time that the interview was over, I had completely forgiven Lex. To be clear, I don't think he was seeking *my* forgiveness, but I realized something important: that while bad things can happen to decent people (bad things can happen to some not-too-decent people, too), it *is* possible to turn things around.

That's truly what Lex Luger has done.

Late in 2017, with *Bischoff on Wrestling* done, I was asked to make an appearance - alongside a varied mix of pro wrestling talent, actors from across the television landscape, and legendary figures from the world of comic books, including Stan Lee - at the new *ACE Comic Con* event in Glendale, Arizona. Billed as "the ultimate fan experience," *ACE* was looking to disrupt the traditional fan-event circuit - defying *convention*, if you will – by promoting their offerings *not* at a convention center, as would typically have been the norm, but rather at the beautiful *Gila River Arena* (now known, incidentally, as the *Desert Diamond Arena*). Its three-day spectacle was to culminate in a final day of festivities on January 15th, 2018, including a wrestling-themed panel discussion and, of course, the customary 'Q & A' session.

In many respects, it was my privilege to be invited - and to participate – especially given that Hulk and Steve Borden, with whom I shared a combined 55 or 60 years of friendship, both agreed to join me on stage. On the other hand, my attitude towards these *kinds* of events (signings, meet and greets, 'Q & As', and the like) remained positively ambivalent – and that's putting it mildly. Prior to this particular convention, I still remember being angry about making public appearances, or simply feeling frustrated that I *had* to do these things – especially, for lack of a better phrase, at this stage of the game.

That's still how I looked at public appearances, quite frankly; not as a potential good time – and certainly not as an 'opportunity' - but rather as something that I *had* to do.

As we got ready to go on stage, I tried to put all that out of my head.

Amanda

14

*Y*ou know what, I thought as the crowd began to cheer our arrival, *this could be fun. There's a great audience out there. This is a great venue, and I'm going up there with Hulk and Sting.*

While I don't remember too much about the bulk of our discussion at the ACE convention, I do remember what happened next. At the end of the 'Q & A' period, a young lady stood up to ask a question – *waaay* out there in the back few rows. There were maybe a thousand people in our section of the venue, so I couldn't quite see her, but I could tell, at least by the sound of her voice, that she was probably in her mid-20's or so.

The young lady got the microphone and said, 'Eric – my name is Amanda. I've always wanted to say this to you, and this is my opportunity.'

Amanda proceeded to tell me that growing up, her family life had been tough. Things had been very challenging in the home, and Amanda didn't get a lot of bonding time with her dad. As a father, that part of her story struck a chord with me immediately - I know just how valuable that time is. Similarly, I also remember being a kid myself, and thinking how much I valued quality time with my *own* dad.

It's really quite important, and therefore, she kind of caught my ear with that. But Amanda went on; she proceeded to say that although

161

she didn't get much time with her dad, there was always one exception: *Monday nights*.

Her father, it turned out, was actually a huge wrestling fan, and very much into the nWo, *Monday Nitro* and everything we were doing in WCW at the time. As a result, young Amanda – wanting to spend time with her dad – became a wrestling fan as well. It ended up becoming the one thing that they shared in common.

I've heard *similar* stories many times before. Fathers come up to me at an autograph signing, their 12-year son in tow, and their *son* wants my autograph. I say to myself, 'Wait a minute – mathematically, this doesn't make any sense. I haven't really been on TV in a long, long time, and the whole WCW/nWo thing happened before…well, you were even a filthy thought in your father's head.' But you hear many stories about how Dad's a wrestling fan, or how different family members sit down to watch wrestling together, and all of a sudden, it becomes a bonding moment.

While on the surface, it would appear that Amanda told me the same kind of story, there was something *especially* touching about how she relayed it – so much so, in fact, that I got a little weepy in front of the crowd.

The moment became kind of a flashpoint for me. After listening to Amanda, I started to think a lot about the impact of her words, and similarly, the impact that perhaps I had - at least, in some small way - being that wrestling was such a cultural force in the '90s. It was on my mind the entire way home.

When I did get home, I told Loree the entire story, but after a couple of days, life took over – and I had other things to worry about. But then one night, maybe about a month later, Loree got an e-mail while we were watching TV in our den. When we're watching TV together, as we often like to do for a couple of hours a night, we usually turn off our phones or ignore them completely - unless it's something really urgent. But evidently, whatever was on Loree's phone, it was important enough that she was reading it intently.

I was trying to watch TV, thinking instead to myself, 'This isn't how we do this, hun!'

But soon Loree looked up and said, 'Oh, wow. Let me read this to you.'

It turned out that through an it's-a-small-world, six degrees of separation kind of thing, Amanda had been able to track down Loree through a mutual acquaintance – and subsequently, she sent her quite a long message.

In her message, Amanda told Loree about how she met me at the Comic-con in Arizona, and about how she had told me about her father. When Loree read that part to me, I immediately went, 'I know who that is – that's Amanda!'

I couldn't have been prepared for what Loree read next. She said that Amanda was .getting married that summer, but her father wouldn't be walking her down the aisle. He had since passed – as had her mother – and consequently, Amanda was hoping that *I* could walk her down the aisle instead.

Even just recounting all of this, it starts to get to me a little bit. It *definitely* got to me when Loree was reading the e-mail.

I took a moment to get myself together.

'Well,' I said to Loree, 'Where are they getting married?'

'Minneapolis,' she replied.

'Hell,' I said, thinking about my own ties to the city. 'Tell her...

'Tell her...*absolutely*. We'll load the dog in the truck...what is it? Twelve hundred miles? It'll be fun. We'll be there.'

By now, it had really started to dawn on me – that what I did, specifically back in the '90s, had such a dramatic impact on so many people (in ways that I would never have imagined). In retrospect, it kind of made sense – I grew up watching wrestling, after all, because my grandmother liked to watch it on Saturday evenings. We only had one TV, and in a real small house, if Grandma wants to watch wrestling, you're gonna watch wrestling!

Well, after watching wrestling for a little bit, all of a sudden, you become a wrestling fan yourself. It happened to me, and it's happened to so many people I know. As stated, I've heard these kinds of stories many times over, but what I didn't ever consider – until Amanda – was just how *important* that can be. That's the part that I missed.

It hit me like a lightning bolt, and the next event I went to, *I thought about all that*. I thought about Amanda, how I first met her, and what her backstory had been. I thought about how much it meant to her that I agreed to walk her down the aisle. It changed the way that I looked at doing live events and signings.

My attitude went from, 'Ugh. I want to kick my own ass for putting myself in a position where I have to do this'-

To, 'Alright, another booking – I get to do another one!'

164

I actually started *looking forward* to being in those places, and once I got there, I had a lot more fun – all because my *attitude* had changed. Amanda's story made me realize that while I was looking at what I did – the competition with WWE and all the successes, failures and challenges that came with it – I viewed my history in the business as transactional. Up until that point, it was just the business that I was in – no more, and no less. Consequently, because it was all transactional, and because it was the business that I was in, I never thought much about the potential positive impact that wrestling can provide, beyond two or three hours of live entertainment.

From that point onwards, I started actually having more conversations with the people that would come up and ask for my autograph. I've always known that in reality, most people don't really want an autograph. Chances are they'll get the autograph, and probably 50% of them will throw it away or lose it within two weeks of getting it. I understand – that's human nature. But what is also human nature, or the real reason why people ask you for an autograph, is based on what they *really want* – that minute or two minutes of direct conversation. They want to feel like they had a chance to get to know you, or perhaps vice versa.

In my experience, that's the psychology behind it, so now, when I started going out to these events, I wouldn't wait for someone to tell me their story - I would *ask* them their story.

'Yeah,' a father would say sometimes in response, 'I got mine watching wrestling when they were five years old.'

It's almost like a father who has a kid playing football: *I got him started when he was five.*

It's all great fun, and I found myself enjoying the engagement so much more. As I found, the more that you engage with people, especially if you are asking questions, the more that they love to tell you. I kept hearing more and more of these amazing stories – not many with as much magnitude as Amanda's – but that's when it really cemented for me.

Man, I thought to myself, *I'm lucky to be doing these things.*

That summer, the day came - and I walked Amanda down the aisle to get married. I remember giving a little speech at the ceremony, and later - knowing she was a wrestling fan – I had Ric Flair surprise her with a congratulatory phone call.

Before we got into position, so to speak, Amanda handed me a hat - emblazoned with the famous 'nWo' logo on the front. There was some writing on the back of the hat, too. It read:

Thanks for standing in for my dad.

Quite naturally, the experience with Amanda got me thinking about my own dad.

I guess we had a close relationship, especially as I got older. When I was younger, in my teenage years especially, I saw my dad as a very, very frustrated and angry person. At the time, I was selfish – I was only concerned about whatever I was trying to do, or trying to buy - a typical teenager, in that respect.

I look at his situation and understand things a lot differently now.

My dad had been a very physical guy: *a tough guy*, you might say. But while he loved being active – hunting, fishing, building things especially – he suffered from terrible, debilitating headaches, stemming from complications arising from his birth as a premature infant. When I was five or six years old, my dad ultimately underwent a brain surgery that did, in fact, alleviate those horrible symptoms; however, he was left without the use of his hands (and with limited use of his arms).

As you might imagine, it was devastating to him, and I became almost akin to his surrogate. My dad would often start these projects around the house – remodeling or building an addition or whatever – but obviously, he couldn't do it anymore himself.

I became his 'hands' - so to speak – but I was a kid, and I wasn't very good at it. My dad was always looking over my shoulder, always frustrated, and he treated me accordingly. That was really tough on me at that age.

At the time, I really didn't understand him. I was thinking, 'God, I'm never gonna get this guy's approval. I can't do anything right.'

That was kind of the way I grew up – always *wanting* my dad's approval, but never really getting it. It wasn't because I was a bad kid, or because I wasn't trying, but it was all due to his constant sense of frustration. This was a guy who couldn't brush his own teeth, couldn't comb his own hair…couldn't take care of himself hygienically. Those kinds of responsibilities now fell all on my mom – and my dad *hated* that.

He took out all that frustration on himself, my mom, and – as the oldest child – me.

By the time I was 16 or 17 years old, I was *out* – I couldn't wait to escape that environment. Whenever possible, I started going off and doing things on my own.

While he may never have said, 'I love you, Eric,' I know that my dad loved me. Once I left home, he was always concerned about me, mainly because I was constantly trying different things. For example, I tried college, but that didn't work out – I just wasn't suited for it. When I was 21 years old, I started what would become one of the biggest commercial landscaping construction companies in Minnesota, and at 22, I bought my first house – in a very desirable area near Lake Minnetonka. Nonetheless, my dad still felt like I was always going to 'blow it'.

He felt that way, at least partially I'm sure, because I would quickly get bored with things. I had built that landscape construction company up, was driving a beautiful car and living in a beautiful home, but soon enough, I got bored with it. I thought to myself, 'Okay – I've done that,' and I sold the business.

My dad asked me why I would do such a thing. He was genuinely puzzled: *What is wrong with you?*

I couldn't really explain things to my dad, other than the fact that I was just bored with it. I wasn't getting up in the morning excited about the company anymore – I wanted to do something else.

So what did I do? I tuned myself into martial arts, of course!

I had enough money, so I trained full time – eight hours a day for about three or four years. As a black belt, I competed as a professional fighter and had two local fights – that is, until I realized there was no money in it. By the time I had that realization, I had kind of gotten bored with that, too.

It set in once I got my black belt, once I had achieved a certain level of success. I thought, 'Okay. Now what?'

I realized that everyone that I trained with – people who were successful in the martial arts – weren't really *that* successful, at least financially. I thought, 'Do I want to own a chain of karate schools in strip malls? Nah – I don't see that either.'

So, in a sense, I abandoned that entire pursuit, too.

I was always good at sales, and quickly, I ended up getting a job as a sales manager for a food processing company. I had about 30 people working for me, and I was very successful at it – until I got bored with that, too.

That's when wrestling showed up in my life.

By the time I started working for Verne Gagne in the AWA – *Controversy Creates Cash* recounts that entire story – I wasn't making a lot of money. I was only making $600 a week, and once Verne and the AWA hit the financial bricks, I wasn't making *anything*. I was going into debt to work there, and things were really tough financially.

Eric, my dad said, *I know you love this wrestling stuff, but how about if I get you a job?*

Despite his condition, my dad had become a very successful, albeit low-level executive for a company called *Cornelius*, a manufacturer of soft drink dispensers (to this day, you can't go into a *Burger King* or a *Taco Bell*, and not see the products that his company manufactured). Even now, whenever I go into a fast food place, I recognize the *Cornelius* logo and think of my dad.

But at the time when the AWA was floundering, he was working really hard to convince me to get "just a regular job."

It doesn't have to be karate or professional wrestling, he would say, *just get a nine-to-five job. I can help you.*

No, Dad, I told him.

I don't want it – I just can't do that.

As per usual, he was entirely frustrated with my response.

Later, when the opportunity came up to work for WCW in Atlanta – my wife and I picked up and moved our family for the job – I think it bothered my dad a lot. He was sad to see us go – sad to see his grandchildren go – and more than anything, he was thinking, 'Oh God, here we go again. He's gonna go down there for a year or two, get bored, and give that job up, too.'

Finally, when I was made Executive Producer – and eventually, Vice President at WCW - my mom and dad decided to come down to Atlanta and visit the kids. Typically, as it was hard for my dad to travel in his condition, we would go up to Minnesota to visit, but for Christmas of 1997, we flew my parents down instead. I thought, 'I'm gonna take my dad over to my office.'

Now, I don't think my dad had any idea how big Turner Broadcasting, WCW's parent company, actually was. He didn't watch CNN – he didn't know what TBS was – he didn't know anything about the *SuperStation*, or anything like that. So I don't know what he was expecting.

When we drove down to CNN Center – to check out my office – a valet greeted me to park the car: *Hi, Mr. Bischoff – how are you?*

My dad looked at me, as if to say, 'Well, this is different.'

We got into the building, and I can still remember my dad's face as he looked around. It was like, 'Holy smokes.' He was genuinely shocked – more shocked than impressed, because he really didn't have any idea previously.

We went up to the famous 14th floor, where my office was, and it was a pretty impressive environment. At this time, I was running the show, and for my dad, I think it made quite the impression on him.

I'll be damned, he probably said to himself.

He's not a fuck up after all!

My dad didn't know how much I was making, but during that visit to Atlanta, he got to see the house we were living in. It was a 2500 square foot home in the suburbs – nothing special, but a little nicer than mid-level income type housing. It was a nice house – he was certainly impressed with it – but Loree and I were living below our means at the time.

Then came the *next* Christmas – 1998 - when we invited my mom and dad to see our new home in Wyoming. We had just finished building it back then, and they hadn't seen any pictures of it –

nothing. I remember meeting them in the driveway, bringing them into the house, and my dad was *stunned*.

Eric, he said, *I have never, in my entire life, seen a home like this.*

I think that's when my dad was *finally* relieved. It was one of the last times that I ever saw him, actually. He died a year-and-a-half later – on July 4th, 2000, my wife's birthday.

I remember that we were out in Wyoming, having just had all the festivities for the holiday and my wife's special day. Loree and I were sitting on the deck of a place that Buffalo Bill Cody actually built – a hotel that he built called *The Irma,* named after his daughter.

It was about six o'clock at night, and I got a phone call from my brother. He let me know that Dad had passed away, during the morning, in his sleep.

I know that my dad was proud of me.

He never said it – he didn't know how to say it – but I know it.

Don't Call It A Comeback

15

For the longest time, my initial foray into podcasting – *Bischoff on Wrestling* – had failed to meet any of my criteria for wanting to do something. It wasn't fun. It wasn't profitable. And it certainly didn't enhance my life in any way. All in all, it hadn't been a good time.

Then, one day, I got a call from Conrad Thompson, whose podcast with WWE executive Bruce Prichard – *Something to Wrestle* – had proven hugely successful. They were making a lot of money with it – *a lot*. I knew that because Bruce told me personally how well they were doing. When I heard it for myself, I said, 'Holy shit – that's serious money. That's not play money. That's serious money.'

I had actually met Conrad somewhere at a convention - maybe a couple years prior to him working with Bruce. While I didn't quite remember the moment, I paid attention when Bruce told me one day, 'You gotta come and meet this Conrad Thompson guy. He'll pay you in cash – a lot of it – and he'll fly you first class to come down to Huntsville, Alabama. He'll pick you up at the airport, bring you out to his house…and you and five or six of his buddies'll sit around and talk wrestling for a few hours.'

Nah, I thought.

I'm good.

'He's got great beer,' continued Bruce. 'Great scotch.'

'You'll really enjoy it,' Bruce petitioned. 'I had a blast doing it, Eric. Come on - you'll really like this guy.'

I eventually relented. *Bruce knows me pretty well*, I thought.

'All right,' I said cautiously. 'I'll give it a whirl.'

At first, everything went as Bruce had described. Conrad picked me up from the airport, and soon, there I was, consuming copious amounts of alcohol with him and about six of his buddies. We were in his man cave when the wrestling talk started.

When I say, 'The wrestling talk started,' I mean that Conrad started *grilling* me.

It was like I was on trial.

Just as soon as I answered one question, it was, 'Well what about this incident?'

And then it was, '*Hmmm*. Well how come you said this, when really this is the truth…'

I found myself thinking, 'This motherfucker is a Dave Meltzer wannabe.'

Bruce was there, by the way, witness to my apparent deposition. I think he must have thought, just by looking at my expression, that things were about to go south. While in general, I don't take a lot of shit, I got through it on this occasion – mostly because I had agreed to be there in the first place.

But don't get me wrong: I was beyond pissed off, and mostly at myself for being in this position. When Conrad drove me back to my hotel, I was more than anxious to get back to Wyoming – as soon as humanly possible (or faster). Once in my room, however, I looked up my flight - only to find it had been canceled.

With not much else to do, I started reflecting on this rather bizarre experience. I thought to myself, 'God damn it - you know you don't like doing this kind of thing.'

By nature, I'm not a very sociable person, and I'm really much more of a loner than people would ever know. I've always been that way. I don't like being around large crowds, for instance, which is really quite ironic given my profession and love of performing. But when I'm out there – in front of the camera – I actually enjoy it, whereas in my personal life, the farther away I am from people that I don't know, the more comfortable I become.

Nonetheless, I had *still* participated in the grilling session - which made thinking about it all the more infuriating.

A couple of months went by until Conrad called me again (I think Bruce might have encouraged him). By this point, *Bischoff on Wrestling* was no more, and quite naturally, Conrad said, 'What do you think about doing a podcast?'

I immediately flashed back to our previous 'conversation' in Conrad's man cave. *I don't know about this*, I thought.

In contrast to my prior podcasting experience, I had no concerns about Conrad's ability to make money with a potential show – clearly, he and Bruce were *printing* money with their own effort.

There were no concerns at all about the business side of the equation. But based on our prior interaction, I wondered what our chemistry would be like 'on-air', so to speak.

I also wanted to know what Conrad had in mind for a prospective format, or simply what we would actually be talking about. I had some respect for what he understood about the business - what he knew already and what he believed could work – and so I wasn't questioning him, *per se*. I was merely trying to understand, for my own benefit, what the approach would be.

'What's the idea?'

'We're gonna go back,' Conrad replied, 'to the *Monday Night Wars*.'

'Oh, Conrad,' I said. 'Nobody wants to hear about that anymore. There's been how many books by how many wrestlers written about it…documentaries that have covered it to death…'shoot interviews' that have been out for years…I don't think anybody wants to hear about it anymore.'

I basically disagreed with Conrad's premise. I said, 'You're wrong.'

What Conrad understood (and at that time, I didn't appreciate) was that nostalgia in wrestling is one of the strongest components of the market. Conrad really 'got' that demo – he had great instincts when it came to that. He knew that for his age group – he was 36 or 37 at the time – the *Monday Night Wars* represented the peak of his wrestling fandom.

I've often been asked about the shelf life of this nostalgia, or why there seems to be a seemingly insatiable appetite, on the part of the wrestling fan, for discussions about the mid-to-late '90s era of wrestling. There are two components at play, I think.

First, wrestling fans – unlike fans of any other 'sport' or spectacle – are probably the most loyal fans in mainstream entertainment. I have no data to back that up, really – it's just based on my experience and therefore, it's a strongly held opinion. Secondly, if you think about those listeners in Conrad's age bracket – people that may now own mortgage companies, like he does, or manufacturing facilities, or real estate companies, or people who are federal judges (I can name them), or people who argue cases before the Supreme Court – they were likely somewhere around their teens (and therefore, were at their most impressionable) when the kind of wrestling that was being produced at that time took place. To them, it will *never* get better than it was at that time of their lives – no matter if somebody in wrestling develops a magic formula that completely transcends the industry, or even if everything was peaking from a creative point of view today. Those people are so loyal to that time period – there's probably a symbiotic relationship between their loyalty and their age – that they just won't be impressed as much as they were in their teens.

They hold on to those memories dearly. It's like when you were the star pitcher on your little league team, or a high school quarterback and you had an undefeated season – all those moments that were so important at those stages of your life are always looked back on so fondly (but wouldn't mean the same if you could put yourself out there again and do it today). But between the fact that wrestling fans are so loyal, and the fact that their adolescence coincided with such an amazing period of time in pro wrestling – it had a profound impact on tens of millions of young people. They *love* listening to stories about that era - especially from the people who were instrumental in making it happen.

In some respects, they're reliving their childhood all over again.

Furthermore, their *kids* now have the opportunity to become fans of that era, due to innovations like the WWE Network and now the content hosted on Peacock. There's such a massive audience for content dissecting that time period, and so many of the key figures from that time are still active today. These factors amount to the *Monday Night Wars* being remembered as being an even bigger deal than it actually was – and it was a big frickin' deal!

With all that in mind, when it came to collaborating with Conrad, I thought, 'You know what. I'm not going to overthink this, or try to out-think somebody that has been very successful with this format. I'm just gonna go with it, and we'll just see what happens.'

I said to Conrad, 'Okay. Let's go ahead and do this, but let's agree that we're only going to do it if it's fun. The minute that it stops being fun is the minute that we stop doing it. That's my criteria. If we can have fun doing this, we're gonna do the podcast for a long time. If we don't have fun doing this, we'll chalk it up as an experiment.'

We decided to call the new show *83 Weeks* – symbolizing WCW's famous winning streak in the ratings war over WWE – and announced that it would launch in May 2018. It would be all wrestling – mostly nostalgia – and most importantly, zero fucking politics.

As for Conrad and I, our first recording ended up as kind of a disaster, at least from my perspective.

I mean, you go back and listen to Episode 1 ("Creating the nWo") of 83 Weeks. It really sounds like I'm giving a deposition. I'm

178

defensive as hell, and definitely have my guard up throughout the conversation. But it wasn't until after the third or fourth episode that the plane, so to speak, almost crashed entirely. While on-air, we actually started yelling at each other – for real – as Conrad began to tire of my uptight responses.

83 Weeks could have ended right there – but we talked about it, agreed to move forward, and slowly, I began to loosen up. I started having fun with the format, learning to laugh at my mistakes and yes, take credit for my successes, too! And despite us still 'ironing out the kinks' early on, the response from the audience was incredible:

New York NY, USA—Westwood One, the largest audio network in the U.S., announces its *83 Weeks with Eric Bischoff* podcast on Westwood One Podcast Network has rocketed to the top of the Apple Podcasts charts every week since it launched in late April. The show had a stellar debut at #1 in the "Sports & Recreation" category and #2 on Apple Podcasts' "Top Podcasts" chart.

Over time, the show led to the creation of a number of catchphrases ('Context is King' would happen to be one of my favorites), various spin-off shows (as in 'Eric Fires Back', where I get to respond to some of the bullshit spouted about yours truly over the years), and the listener-supported *AdFreeShows.com* (close to 4000 subscribers strong). As of the time of this writing, *83 Weeks* – now four-and-a-half years into its run – has been a phenomenal success (with up to 150,000 downloads on a weekly basis).

Having said all of that, I honestly never thought that *83 Weeks* would stay around for so long. I figured, 'Okay, once we cover those weeks – when *Nitro* was beating *Raw* in the ratings – what else are we going to talk about?' That was kind of a dilemma for me, so I asked someone that I had met in New York – a voice coach with a lot of knowledge about podcasting and radio – to take a listen and let me know her opinion on what we were doing. She had some feedback about a few technical things, but my biggest takeaway was her

179

advice about how to give the podcast some longevity. She said, 'You need to figure out a way to make what you're talking about *relevant* to today. Find two or three times in each show to highlight a relevance between the topic and what people are watching today, or what is happening in the industry currently. Do that and people will always listen.'

That advice really stuck with me. Whenever I get the show notes in advance of an episode (sometimes I read them, most of the time I don't), I try to think about how to apply that guidance. I also don't like to have prepared answers for anything that Conrad is going to ask me, because to me, that approach doesn't come off as genuine or authentic. If I have time to think about *how* to answer a question, I also tend to overthink my answers, and it just doesn't feel the same. But more than anything, I look for those opportunities to draw parallels between the past and the present. It gives the show more 'legs', so to speak, and that's one way that *83 Weeks* has stayed relevant.

The other technique that I've grown to utilize is humor. A few years ago, I started reading and studying comedy writers, wanting to know how they come up with their material. I'm fascinated by the process that goes into it, the formulas that they employ in leading you to a punchline. I thought, 'There's an application here to the podcast world, too.' If people are laughing while they're listening, then we're entertaining them as well as informing them. I don't want to make it sound like I'm trying to be a comedian, because I'm not – but I always look for ways to add levels of humor to the show.

Finding humor also helps deal with some of the negativity that comes from covering my tenure in the business, or simply dealing with the nature of the business in general. Often, I'll respond to something that has been written about me by making light of it in a non-disparaging way. Rather than get defensive, I'll just tear into a *mucker futher* and have fun doing it.

When we first started talking about doing *83 Weeks*, I wasn't particularly interested in answering the familiar criticisms about the 'rise and fall' of WCW, especially with respect to some of the booking decisions that have been so thoroughly discussed over the years. What people may not always appreciate is that back then, we weren't producing the content with the expectation that years later, other people would be dissecting the intricacies of that content over a two- or three-hour podcast.

Conversely, it is interesting to consider that today's performers and producers might already have an awareness that years from now, there will likely be similar long-form, retrospective and often critical analysis of their *own* creative output. Then again, while this is going to sound like I'm patting myself on the back, I don't think wrestling is making nearly as big an impression on the people watching it today as those who followed it back then. I think much of the audience today is watching it passively – it's something to do other than watching the news, or maybe a scripted drama, and I don't think the level of passion in today's product is going to translate to the same kind of audience (in podcasting, or whatever the next iteration of media will be) in the future.

I don't necessarily see what there'll be to talk about. Pro wrestling has become more akin to Olympic gymnastics, or figure skating than anything else. It's very aesthetic; it's dynamic as hell; it's colorful…but the characters are not there. They're just not. You look at whoever the heavyweight champion is of any wrestling company in the country, at any given moment, and *sure* – they're technically in that role – but they don't have a fraction of the impact of 'Stone Cold' Steve Austin, or Hulk Hogan, or The Rock, or Bill Goldberg, for that matter.

When I broke into the wrestling business in 1987, I was not allowed to go anywhere *near* the creative side of wrestling. Verne Gagne was very, very strict about *kayfabe*, and unless you absolutely needed to know something to do your job, you were not allowed anywhere near it. That's how I was introduced to the business – working for a wrestling company, but still being able to enjoy the mystique of it all. I would often wonder to myself, 'How are they gonna be able to pull this off?' – and I worked there!

It's not like I believed any of it was real, but it didn't matter, because the magic was how it looked real - how it *felt* real. In large part, that feeling was due to the performances, for lack of a better word. The characters back then had developed over a long period of time, gaining experience in various regions and territories. Dusty Rhodes didn't just wake up one morning and say, 'Hey, I'm going to do this and be Dusty Rhodes.' All of the guys that we remember so vividly learned how to be their characters in a *real-world environment*.

They would sometimes go out and fail – imagine that – because they would try something new in front of a live crowd. But then the next night, they would try something a little different, and after seeing that it worked, they would add that little wrinkle to their repertoire. Over the course of 10, 12, 15 years, their characters emerged 'without a net' – in a situation where you *have* to get good at it.

Fast forward to today, and you simply don't have that. You have some talent that has developed some skills, often coming from the independent scene, but very few of them – if any – have the same level of *ownership* over their character. Very few of them, if any, have the potential of becoming The Rock or Hulk Hogan.

They simply didn't come up in the same industry, wherein characters developed in front of a live audience – not a sterile practice or training environment, as is so often the case today – while

182

learning instinctively what works and what doesn't. Therefore, it doesn't feel *real* anymore; it feels rehearsed – which it is.

All they're doing is going out and *pretending* that they're wrestlers.

Oh, I've heard all the arguments. I've heard all the claims that *external* factors are mostly responsible for the (relative) lack of interest in wrestling today (as compared to the *Monday Night War* era). There are so many more entertainment options, they say – and I get it. Mass media has become so much more fragmented – agreed. People are watching the shows with a smartphone in hand – correct.

But if you want to know the truth, the people who blame the state of today's industry on technological changes (namely streaming), or worse yet, those who swear today's product is "better than ever" – it's just that the world has changed, you see – well, those people are lying to themselves.

It's like somebody who smokes three packs of cigarettes a day, but attributes their inability to run five miles on the fact that they don't have a really good pair of running shoes. No – it's the fact that you smoke three packs of cigarettes a day!

It's so easy to make excuses, or to convince yourself of something that isn't actually rooted in reality. Let's think about something for a minute.

In late 2007 to early 2008, there was the Writers Guild of America strike, the effect of which led to the rise of 'non-scripted' (reality) television. Simply from an economic perspective, television studios and networks needed content, and clearly, they couldn't hire any writers – because they were on strike – and Directors, showing solidarity with the writers, wouldn't direct anything.

Scripted entertainment in Hollywood *died*. All over town, there were people on the ledge of their apartment buildings, drinking cocktails and thinking about taking a dive. According to Hollywood, non-scripted television would dominate the future of entertainment. Everyone kind of bought into a version of that argument, and they all said, 'Okay – it's *Who Wants To Be A Millionaire…Survivor…Dancing with the Stars* from here on out.'

'The business has changed,' they all said. 'The world has changed. Reality TV has changed everything!'

Almost without exception, they all thought scripted television was dead…until *Breaking Bad* came along.

It's the same parallel conversation that people are having today about streaming platforms: *everything has changed!*

But when *Breaking Bad* broke on the scene - with the strike (incidentally enough) almost coming to an end - people started realizing something: the viewing audience was hungry for a great *story*. What's the lesson here? If the story is good, it will work. If the characters are good, it will work – just like *The Walking Dead*, or *Vikings*, or any number of amazing scripted shows that have emerged since *Breaking Bad*.

The minute that those in wrestling learn what the moral of the story is – that people want great story and character development – wrestling will make a huge comeback. But if the status quo remains – in my opinion - there's just not going to be a large enough base of people that care about today's wrestling, in order for it to be discussed on a commercial basis for years at a time (as in the case of *83 Weeks*). It's all just kind of bland right now. It's all just kind of 'meh.'

Then again, if today's wrestling *does* inspire a series of retrospective podcasts 20 years from now, I'm sure that Conrad will have something to do with it.

Today, I would consider Conrad one of my closest friends. He and I are probably as closely aligned as entrepreneurs – in terms of our instincts and goals – as anybody that I've ever worked with, other than perhaps Jason Hervey. We just complement each other really well – it's a symbiotic kind of relationship. In certain areas, I have more experience than he does, but in turn, he possesses certain strengths that I don't necessarily have. He balances out some areas where I don't have a lot of experience, or areas that are just flat-out weaknesses for me. I'm certainly willing to admit I have weaknesses, by the way – there's no 'shame in my game' when it comes to that.

We have fun trying new ideas, and exploring new opportunities. We recently launched a limited series on local radio, because we thought, 'Everybody in the radio industry is moving into the podcast world – because that's where the money is – but *surely* that means there's a void for content on radio'. We kind of reversed engineered ourselves into a radio show for a short time. Those kinds of opportunities will continue to emerge - as long as we're still willing to try new things.

As a business, *AdFreeShows* (our paid platform) generates in excess of $1,000,000 on an annual basis, and that doesn't include what each of the podcasts on that platform generates, which I'll estimate at an average of about $25,000 or $30,000 a month each. So that's kind of a big business. At this point, we have our own internal ad sales

185

team, and probably half to three-quarters of the ads on all of our respective podcasts are generated in-house. In developing our own ad sales team, we can dramatically grow revenue, in large part because we're driving ads for *ourselves* – companies and products we have involvement in – versus driving ads for other people.

Personally, I interact a lot with the subscribers of *AdFreeShows*. I see them more as friends or family members, really, and some of them have come out to Wyoming to have a beer with me – to come and visit my house even. Then, most days, right after dinner – when I'm taking my dog for her evening hike – Conrad will usually call, and we'll kind of riff together back and forth. We never have an agenda or anything like that, but we share what I call 'What if?' kind of ideas. That's a really fun process for me – in fact, any conversation that starts with that question immediately gets my attention.

When you start a conversation with a question, it tends to open up the mind a lot more. Back in the WCW days, I didn't have quite as strong a handle on this as I do now, but if you look at most wrestling angles or stories, they start out with a statement: *Wrestler A has broken into an interview and hit Wrestler B in the head with a chair.* Nobody asks the interesting questions, as in the obvious one: *Why did he do that?*

I used to tell the announcers all the time: when you're on commentary, *ask questions*. Don't act like you know everything. If you're asking questions, and the audience is hearing you ask questions, guess what? They're going to try and answer those questions. They're going to talk about those questions. They're going to ask their friends what they think about those questions.

That's how you create a 'buzz' around a particular storyline or story development, by asking and creating questions. 'Who's The Third Man?' was the perfect example of that – it was the biggest question in wrestling at that time, and that's how I learned about it. I said, 'God, that really works. Let's ask the fans: is he a good guy - or is he a bad guy?'

Creating *questions* creates interest, and making *statements* often doesn't.

With that being said, I think I heard enough questions – in Conrad's fucking man cave – to last me a lifetime.

Controversy Still Creates Cash

16

I've often been asked if the statement 'Controversy Creates Cash' still holds true.

I would suggest that it's *truer* today than it was when I wrote the book with that tagline - in all aspects of life.

Let's look at social media, which is *driven* by controversy. The content that receives the most attention is, to one degree or another, combative, seeking attention and creating controversy in order to accomplish that. I think if you look at so much of what's driving our culture - and our politics reflect our culture in many aspects - it's *driven* by controversy.

Controversy creates emotion, and people *act* on emotion - unfortunately. I think the world would be a better place if people responded to things more on an intellectual level, but our news media is more like professional wrestling than professional wrestling is! It's all designed to create emotion.

Having spent time in North Korea, I can tell you first-hand what happens to a population when they're closed off from outside ideas, outside information or outside knowledge. They get fed a steady diet of state-run propaganda – presented to them as 'the news' – but in the United States, while we have a completely different system, an all-too-obvious phenomena is happening here, too. Almost everything in our culture is driven by the mass media, which creates controversy in order to create a desired emotion – either to get people to want to watch something, buy the product that's being advertised while they watch, or to get certain people elected.

I've been discussing this subject for a long time. In December 2006, I posted the following observations at *EricBischoff.com*:

"The American people know (insert a political agenda here so that it sounds like the speaker is wired directly into the minds of 300+ million people like some kind of Super Nielson Consciousness Meter)"

...We've heard that phrase – *The American people know* - thousands of times. It's one of the most over-used yet effective means of swaying public opinion. Don't believe me? Just listen to CNN and almost any democrat running for office or speaking on behalf of their party. Democrats are always anxious to step in front of a microphone and speak on behalf of "The American People".

The problem is.... I'm an American and the democratic party and those who represent them, rarely espouse a position that is close to one that I hold. Yet they claim to speak for me. Don't get me wrong, if I hear the words "The American people know...." coming out of the mouth of a republican....it drives me just as crazy. It's presumptuous, arrogant, and elitist. But unfortunately, it is also effective, because it attracts the disaffected (and most vocal) members of society, and that special breed of parasite that feeds off of them.

It's gotten even worse since then. The people that produce news media know that people react based on emotion – they don't react based on thought. They don't think about *why* they are reacting the way that they are, they're just justifying the way that they *feel*, based on whatever they've read or whatever they subscribe to.

Any political system that's driven, at its core, by controversy, is likely to be characterized by much of the volatility we see today.

190

Once upon a time - when Loree and I were living part of the year in Cave Creek, Arizona - I found myself following the local political scene.

Cave Creek is a beautiful little community – home to about 5,000 residents or so – and it's successfully retained a lot of its Western heritage (during the late 1800's, it became somewhat of a 'boom town' after gold was discovered in the Bradshaw Mountains). You can actually ride a horse into town, as I often did - making use of the trails that go through the downtown area - and actually 'park' your horse outside a bar or a restaurant (using the corrals that are plentiful in that area).

Shortly after we moved to town, however, a lot of new construction got underway – condominiums and hotels primarily. It looked like the community was going to rapidly change - at the cost, I worried, of the charm, warmth and quaintness that attracted people there in the first place. As the subject was being discussed at the local town council meetings, I decided to stick my head in the door and witness the process for myself.

It was *ridiculous*. After I saw the process, and in particular the type of people that comprise these town council meetings, I knew that I didn't have the patience for it.

Thus ended my brief flirtation with politics.

In late 2018, I was approached by the promoter of a *Tedx* talk in Naperville, Illinois. He reached out to me and said, 'I think your story is really interesting, and your book is, too. I think you've got a unique take on certain things, and we've never had a talk with somebody from the wrestling industry. You can talk about anything you want – we'd love to have you.'

I had never watched a *Ted* talk, or a *Tedx* talk in this case, prior to being involved with one myself. I was aware of them – and how popular they have become online – but I was just never motivated to sit down and watch one. But in preparation for my own talk, I went back and watched the ones that were really successful - as well as the ones that absolutely bombed. As with everything else, I wanted to understand why certain talks worked, and why others didn't. I wanted to understand the formula, because when speaking in front of a large group, it's easy to lose people. You get a golden opportunity in the first 15 or 30 seconds that you're out there to grab their attention, but if you don't *keep* their attention and have your shit together, it's very easy to lose them. People have other things going on, everybody's got a smartphone now, and they can *pretend* that they're listening while really doing something else. I didn't want that.

So I worked on the talk for quite a while, jotting down notes and trying out some ideas in my head. I really wanted to make a good impression, and a few days before the big day, the producer asked if I could send across my presentation. There's a very specific window in which you can deliver a talk in this format, but I had it all timed out already. I made sure I felt comfortable with it, walked through it myself at home – before I got on the plane – because I knew there'd be pauses and reactions to what I was saying. I tried to anticipate those reactions so that I would come in *exactly* on time – just like we do in wrestling.

I took a plane to Chicago, about 30 miles from Naperville, and continued the editing process on board. I was busy working on my iPad, cleaning things up, changing a word here or there, fine-tuning things as best as I could. Before long, however, it was starting to get late - my flight had been delayed (big surprise to anyone who has flown recently. It's even worse now.) – and the next thing I knew, the flight attendant was coming by to wake me up.

In a bit of a daze, I grabbed my bag from overhead and hustled out the door, anxious to get to my hotel, take a shower, and wake up in the morning to finish my speech. Well, when I woke up that morning to finish the speech, I didn't have it anymore - my iPad, evidently, had been left on the plane.

I know, I know. You're supposed to have these things 'backed up', right? Well, I didn't. As a result, I couldn't just call Loree and ask her to forward me the presentation - at least, the version before my most recent edits on the plane.

Nope - it was *gone*.

What in the fuck, I initially thought to myself, *are you gonna do now?*

I had worked on the speech long enough that it was still kind of in my head. I probably could have gotten *close* to achieving the reaction that I wanted, even if it wouldn't have been perfect. But rather than agonize over what to do, I kind of shrugged and said to myself, 'You know what – fuck it. I'm just gonna 'improv' it.'

I decided that I was going to talk about politics (having successfully avoided the subject all year on *83 Weeks*); and specifically, how the arena of politics had come to exhibit many of the characteristics that were once associated with professional wrestling. After all, our politics, I have often thought, is nothing more than a reflection of our *culture*, of which wrestling has been quite influential. To bring the point home, I thought, I would use examples to show how these worlds have converged over time.

The link was blatantly obvious to me, but not so obvious to most people who don't take wrestling seriously, or simply just don't watch it. I knew that I could make it work, because it's honestly how I feel - and I think about these things a lot. I try to be analytical with respect to what I see going on around me. I ask myself questions like, 'Why is it like this? Why is someone saying this? Why is this particular policy being proposed?'

Now I was excited - but I still needed a way to get the audience's attention.

Soon a smile came across my face.

I'm a wrestling guy, I thought. *Why not just cut a heel promo?*

I can assure you, with absolute certainty, that nobody has ever come out on any kind of *Ted* talk and started ripping on the producer of the talk, the city that it's situated in, or the people sitting close to the stage. Nobody has ever done that, but that's how I decided to get their attention – to get them to *feel* so uncomfortable that they couldn't take their eyes off me.

About five minutes before it was my time to go out – as they were 'micing' me up backstage – I called the producer over.

I'm gonna go out there, I told him, *and do something that will make you – for a brief, fleeting moment – want to send security out there to get me off the stage.*

I just want to assure you, I continued, *that everything is going to be fine. People are really going to enjoy it – at least in the end.*

I stepped on stage to applause, looking less than enthused with the crowd's reaction:

194

Is that all you got? Seriously, I'm a little disappointed. No, it's not funny. I flew all the way here from Los Angeles – it took me an entire freaking day to get here – and I get this Pavlovian dog response…because you feel like you're supposed to be polite.

…I am one of the most important people that you're gonna see on this stage today – and by far, the best looking!

…What are you smiling about? And look at you. You wanna come up here and take me off the stage? By all means…I'll wait.

…This town sucks. The only people who think Naperville is a great town are people that have never been anywhere else.

…And this building…are you kidding me? Salvation Army not available, maybe?

…Wipe that look off your face, lady. I know what you're thinking. I'm busy tonight – forget about it!

If you go back and watch the talk online, you can witness the audience go mostly silent for almost three minutes of my 'Act 1' (albeit with some uncomfortable laughter sprinkled in). It turned out to be a pretty powerful experience - they didn't recognize at all what I was doing.

But now I had them - I had their full attention. There wasn't anyone in that place who could even utter a syllable, nor was there anyone pretending to listen, while sitting and staring at their phone instead. It was time to transition to 'Act 2':

Alright, I'm glad this part is over!

…Had I continued, and gone further in trying to make you all hate me…the very next person who would've come out here…would more than likely have gotten a standing ovation. That means I would've done my job…because that's what I do.

…People don't realize just how enduring professional wrestling is in our culture.

…When it comes to content…professional wrestling and the news are the two most enduring forms of content that there are. Before the night is over, I'm going to try and convince you they're far more similar than you think.

I started drawing the connection between wrestling, its ability to create emotion, and how the news media – and subsequently our political climate – is driven by emotion as well:

Verne Gagne was a professional wrestling promoter in Minneapolis who hired me…

…One of the first things he taught me was…when it comes to the audience, it doesn't really matter if they love a wrestler – or hate them. As long as they feel passionately – one way or another – business would be good.

…Professional wrestling was one of the first weekly network television shows back in the 1950's – at the beginning of the television age. It went from there to being the number one local television show – long before cable came around – in any city in the United States.

…Cable television came along…and professional wrestling became – and still is, to this day – the most watched form of weekly entertainment. The digital age…WWE has 25 million fans around the world. They have a market cap of $6 billion, and they trade on the New York Stock Exchange for right around 75, 78 dollars – depending on the day.

How did it get so big? How did professional wrestling become such a big part of our culture?

It's simple. They don't make you think – it's not like a Ted talk - they make you *feel*.

…It wasn't until after I got out of the wrestling business, that I realized that the news media – and politicians as well – use much of the same formula. They don't want you to think – they want you to feel.

As long as you feel passionately – one way or another – business is good.

For most people, I would argue, facts, knowledge and information are boring, and they certainly don't create emotion. People are hooked on emotion.

This might sound weird, but some people *love* to hate, and some people *love* being afraid, too. These strong emotions can be as addictive as love itself, or the more positive feelings that may arise about someone or something.

I continued:

What you're watching television isn't so much informing you – and making you think – it's making you feel…and pissing you off, more than often than not. That's what they wanna do – it's called 'cheap heat' in the wrestling business. It's easy…just like me coming out here and making fun of people…it's easy to get people to react to that kind of thing. It's a lot easier to get people to react than asking them to think. That's what they do.

…Ted Turner launched CNN, the first cable news outlet…24 hours, international news – that was Ted's vision. Ted believed he could bring the world closer together as a result of that – but here's what happened. Fox followed him, MSNBC followed the business model, and what they realized is that it's a helluva lot cheaper to put 3 or 4 'talking heads' in the studio – talking about the news and giving opinions about the news – than it is going out, and actually reporting it.

…Now what you see, when you're looking for information, are 'talking heads' *arguing*. No matter what it is, they're gonna find a way to argue about it.

It's kind of crazy, when you think about it.

For the finale, my 'Act 3' if you will, I asked the audience to consider an intriguing question:

What if I told you, right now, that there is a very good chance that many of you in this room will vote for a professional wrestler to be the next President of the United States? You laugh? Donald Trump is in the WWE Hall of Fame. Let that sink in. Now he wasn't a professional wrestler…but just recognize…not only is the current President of the United States in the WWE Hall of Fame, a member of his cabinet – Linda McMahon, the former CEO of WWE – heads up the Small Business Administration.

…If I'm right, and you all do vote for a professional wrestler to become the next President of the United States, it might just be history repeating itself – and it might not be all that bad.

Believe it or not, Abraham Lincoln – one of this country's greatest Presidents – was at one time, before he became a lawyer, a professional wrestler.

It can happen! Thank you all very much.

I left the stage to a standing ovation – the talk had been a great success. I was taking in the compliments and looking forward to a cocktail when a journalist from Chicago approached me backstage. He was *pissed*.

In his mind, I had basically disparaged the majority of journalists today, including him. He almost spoke as if I had personally attacked him, or that I had implied that everyone in his business was doing the exact same thing – as if there was some kind of factory from which they came from.

We ended up having a long discussion. I knew that there was no way I was going to change his mind – he was too entrenched in his ideology, quite honestly – but I was just hoping to get him to say, 'Okay, I don't agree with you – but I understand it.' I figured that would be a really big win for me.

There were certain current events that we debated, things that everybody had recognized as being lies, falsehoods or exploitation on the part of those in the news media.

I guess we'll agree to disagree, he eventually conceded.

198

I hadn't changed his mind – far from it, in fact – but he was no longer angry.

He was thinking – not feeling – and that was good enough for me.

Beverly Hillbillies

17

As of the time of this writing, Loree and I have been married for 38 years. It's been quite the journey for both of us.

I was 27 when we met – six years older than she was – but honestly, we were probably the same age emotionally (that's not uncommon, by the way - men mature, in my opinion, at a rate much slower than women). We were both *kids*, really – but Loree, even back then, was a far more enlightened person than I was. She pushed us to make a commitment that became kind of our mantra: *no matter what, let's always have fun.*

No matter how tough things were for us – and believe me, they were miserable in the days before I worked for WCW – that commitment kept us going. We would say to each other, 'Okay – things are bad, but you know what? It's Friday night. Let's go *stay* in love with each other.'

Like everybody else, we called those nights our 'date nights' - but in our case, I actually *treated* her as if we were on a date. It wasn't simply, 'We're a married couple having a date night. Let's try and escape the realities of our week,' it was, 'Let's have some real fun.'

And we did. We always had a lot of fun, and we always made an effort to enjoy everything that comes with that – intimacy included.

As a result, I often joke, we have been 'dating' each other for our entire relationship.

In terms of her approach to life, Loree has advanced as far as anybody that I've ever known. There's a lot to learn about the way she approaches life. She would always tell me, 'Eric, don't be angry about things in the past,' or 'Don't hold on to the negative things.'

She would say, 'Don't worry about what's going to happen next month, or next year, or five years from now. Let's enjoy the day – let's be grateful for whatever it is we have.'

Intellectually, I always understood what her position was: *Yeah, I get it – I should feel grateful for being able to wake up today; for being healthy.* I could process all of that, but I couldn't *relate* to it personally – until I got a dog.

A dog named Nickie.

Let me backup a little bit - it all *really* started with a dog named Stevie.

Stevie was an Australian cattle dog – a *Velcro dog,* as owners of the breed will surely attest to. Anyone with experience around these dogs will know about their loyalty, which is typically directed towards one person, and their intelligence, which is typically off-the-charts.

I've been around dogs all my life - I actually worked in an animal hospital when I was a teenager - but I had *never* met a dog like Stevie. I absolutely fell in love with her.

I kept her with me 24 hours a day, seven days a week. If I had to travel, it would tear my guts up that I had to leave her behind.

One such occasion happened in 2016 - when both Loree and I had to leave town (Cave Creek, Arizona at that time of year) on business. I boarded Stevie with a lady with whom I had boarded her before. The lady had a big, beautiful home – high fences and everything – a perfect set-up for boarding dogs like ours. While I always hated dropping Stevie off with someone else, I felt as comfortable as I could in doing so there.

As we were both flying out the next morning, Loree and I then went out for a bite to eat. My phone soon rang with a call from the lady.

Eric, uh…where's Stevie?

I was incredulous.

What do you mean, 'Where's Stevie?'

I dropped her off – she's there!

Well, she responded, *I don't see her.*

I can't find her, Eric.

Jumping immediately back in my truck, I bolted back towards where I had just left Stevie – a paltry three-mile drive from the restaurant. I was gunning it as fast as possible when my phone rang in the truck.

It was a phone number I didn't recognize – and soon a voice I had never heard before.

Hey, said the person – evidently another lady who had encountered Stevie - *are you missing your dog?*

I was elated.

Yes!

Oh my God, I thought. *Somebody has found Stevie.*

I'm so sorry, she quickly interjected. *I just found her.*

She's dead on the side of the road.

I can't even really describe how I felt at that moment – something akin to shock, for sure. It was a horrible, horrible moment for me.

I drove over to meet the lady who had found Stevie (my phone number was displayed on her tag), and indeed, there Stevie was – dead on the side of the road. I put her in my truck and turned back towards the boarding house. Once I got back there, things got *ugly* – and fast.

Still in shock, I found myself saying and doing things that I would certainly regret later on. There was nothing physical, of course - nothing like that - but by the time I got home, the Sheriffs were at the house waiting for me.

Things got even uglier.

My dog had just been found dead, but apparently, *I* was the one being questioned. Needless to say, that fucking pissed me off. I hadn't done anything illegal. I hadn't threatened anybody – or anything like that.

I was angry - and I was hurt.

Although I didn't want to, I had to get up – the situation with the Sheriffs now thankfully resolved – in order to go to the airport the next day. I was still devastated, but I felt an obligation to inform the breeder – a lady named Kim Robinson – about what had happened to Stevie.

I called up Kim but could hardly get the words out. I was a wreck, sitting there in that airport, crying like a child, trying my best to communicate with her. She could hear in my voice how upset I was.

Eric, I have a dog that's the pick of the litter. I was going to keep it for myself, but I'm going to hold her for you. Whenever you're ready, she'll be here for you.

While I was taken aback at Kim's kindness, I couldn't really think clearly in that moment. There was no way, as far as I was concerned, that another dog could even approach filling the void that I was feeling. I didn't even think it was *possible* to have a relationship like I had with Stevie.

But it was getting close to the time of year – the middle of May, typically – when Loree and I would load up the horses, load up my Harley, put everything in a trailer and drive out from Arizona to our home in Wyoming. If we wanted to take care of another dog, now was the time to make a decision; therefore, finally, we opted to travel to a different destination first: Portland, Oregon, in order to pick up *Nickie*.

Kim had been sending me pictures of Nickie for the prior two months, and I couldn't wait to go and pick her up. At the same time, I was still devastated over Stevie, and I worried about how this might come out in front of the breeder. I didn't want to break down or fall apart in front of people that I didn't really know – that's kind of weird at the best of times. But then, once we got to the breeder's house, I saw Nickie in person for the first time.

I fell apart.

To tell you the truth, I'm on the verge of falling apart as I think about it now.

Just like Stevie, Nickie is now with me '24/7' – and she's always excited to start the day. This is how it usually goes: she'll wake me up as soon as the sun starts rising – as soon as there's even a crack of light. I'll get up, sit on the deck with my cup of coffee, and Nickie will sit there at my feet - just kind of stoically looking out over the property, looking out off into the distance. It's such a peaceful way to start the day.

Once the sun is up, I'll go take her for a hike – sometimes half an hour, sometimes two hours – and I'll watch her run around in her element (Australian cattle dogs, like Nickie, are very high energy and physical – they were bred to herd cattle, after all, in some of the most rugged parts of the world). As I watch her chase some rabbits or deer around, I find myself, in some respects, living vicariously through her. It really helps clear my head before starting the day.

I don't know if I fully appreciated the power of a great dog until Stevie and Nickie (so named after Stevie Nicks, by the way) came into our lives. You get to experience unconditional love on a constant basis, and you learn something from them every single day.

A great dog appreciates the basic things in life. They don't judge. They don't care about whatever is going on with your personal or professional life – good or bad. If you give them love, companionship and direction, they're the most loyal, forgiving, loving animals on the face of the earth.

I don't have a shrink, but I have a great dog, and I think that serves just as well.

While I'm off taking Nickie for a hike, Loree is usually reading or meditating (after I've delivered her customary cup of coffee, that is). She's the reason why we have such a positive pattern in our lives – nobody, as a general rule, wakes up in our house in a bad mood.

My wife is tough as hell. You would have to work really hard, from a mental and emotional standpoint, to get 'Mrs. B' off her game. In terms of being positive, looking for a silver lining, or looking for an opportunity to turn things around, that mindset is in her *nature*. It has only become more impressive to me as the years have gone by.

She's become a voracious reader. If you were to look into our bedroom, there's probably a stack of four or five hardcovers on her night stand, and two walls of books that she's read over the last year or two – almost all of them relating to health, wellness, spirituality and controlling one's emotions.

As I look back on the stresses and challenges that have occurred throughout our lives, I didn't handle them anywhere near as well as she did. To get through those times, I found myself leaning on Loree a lot, and she was really my guide throughout some of the very lowest of times. She helped me recognize moments in which my aggressive nature – more often than not an asset in the wrestling business – was actually working *against* me, and how to harness it more positively.

She's steady as a rock. She just doesn't waver. She has plenty of experience in dealing with change.

We would soon face a change that no-one could have predicted.

In May 2019, I got a call from Bruce Prichard – Vince McMahon's long-time 'right hand man' – who had recently returned to WWE. After ten years away from the company, Bruce had been appointed to WWE's creative team in February, but within a month, he was promoted to the Senior Vice President level. I was surprised that he had the time to call me.

Hey, Eric, Bruce said, *there are some big changes going on here.*

Would you be interested in coming back?

I guess I could have been excused for thinking that 'coming back' meant returning to WWE as a *talent* – after all, my run as General Manager had been extremely successful (I didn't even see it lasting 90 days, let alone three-and-a-half years). But that run was over a decade ago.

Not just as a talent, Bruce clarified.

Would you be interested in coming to work here - to help with the direction that we're going?

I didn't even think about it, nor did I ask any questions. I didn't even ask what the role was.

Sure, Bruce, I replied in amazement, *if there's a spot for me that makes sense.*

I suppose it was the kid in me – the 35-year-old in me. I didn't give it any second thought. The prospect of collaborating again with Bruce was almost enough for me, quite frankly. During our time in TNA – despite all of the shit that was going on around us – we had complemented each other perfectly. We often had contrasting opinions about things, but we developed the ability to take those contrasting opinions, and actually come up with something better – collectively – than would have individually been possible. It was one of the things that I missed – having a great idea, sitting down in a room with someone or a group of people, and having that idea challenged (and progressed) in a constructive way. I missed that energy, and quite honestly, I missed that part of the business.

Two days later, I got another phone call – this time from Brad Blum, Vince's Chief of Staff – and the next thing I knew, I was on a plane for the first of two meetings with Brad and Vince himself.

I don't know what was going on in Vince's head – I don't think anybody does – but I do remember how I was feeling. As far as I was concerned, there was no way in which I wasn't getting the job. I didn't see anyone else out there with the qualifications that I had, and my previous experience with WWE – albeit working strictly as a talent – had been a positive experience for everyone involved.

While granted, Vince knew me as the guy who competed against him – the guy who almost put him out of business – he also knew me as a team player, because as a talent, I would basically not question anything I was asked to do – unless I had an idea to possibly make it better. Even in those circumstances, my tone was more along the lines of, 'Hey, I've got an idea, so if this works – great. If not, let's do *your* thing.'

When I walked into the room for the first meeting, it was like seeing a buddy from college that I hadn't seen in years – there was none of the typical angst, anxiety or stress that would normally go into that kind of a meeting. I don't want to give the impression that Vince and I are friends – or *were* friends prior to that meeting – but there was certainly a mutual respect there.

I went in there with confidence, both in myself and my perspective on what WWE needed at that point in time. I had thought about the subject for so many years – and talked about it on avenues such as *83 Weeks* – that I didn't really have to 'prep' much for anything. At the risk of sounding flippant about it, I didn't feel any pressure about having to impress Vince in order to get hired.

On a similar note, my life didn't depend on whether or not I got the job, either. *If it works out*, I thought, *great – I'll be happy. If it doesn't work out, I'll go back to my great life – no problem.* I was doing a lot of other things that were occupying my time, including a movie project that was just getting set up with *Netflix*. As part of that project – a biopic recounting the career of Hulk Hogan - I was looking at the opportunity to work with people like Todd Phillips (director of *Joker* and *The Hangover* series of films, among many others) and Scott Silver (screenwriter of *Joker*, *8 Mile* and *The Fighter* - just to name a few). There was plenty on the horizon to get excited about – even if that excluded WWE.

210

At the second meeting – in which only Vince, Brad and myself attended – I learned more about the supposed new direction. The vision, as it was explained to me, was for Paul Heyman and Eric Bischoff to become 'Executive Directors' (WWE's in-house title for the position of 'Showrunner', for all intents and purposes) of *Raw* and *Smackdown* respectively. As such, I would be expected to oversee all elements pertaining to the *Smackdown* show - including creative, marketing, promotion, licensing, and the integration of all of the above.

It was a big, big job. *Smackdown* was just months away from debuting on the Fox network, by virtue of a five-year ($1 billion) agreement it reached with WWE during the previous summer. The first episode on Fox – scheduled to occur on October 4th, 2019 – would also take billing as the show's *20th Anniversary* special. Moreover, the episode was set to become the first WWE programming to air on Fox in 27 years.

Similar to my previous conversations on the subject, I didn't ask a lot of questions. Vince offered me the job – we had a big hug - and I was excited as all hell. I was still processing it all when on my way out, I bumped into Stephanie McMahon in the elevator.

Oh! she laughed as we made eye contact.

*Why am I not surprised to see **you** here?*

The new role promised not only the chance to work with Bruce again, but the opportunity for direct, one-on-one communication with Vince himself.

I had never had that before. While I worked with Vince creatively - for segments that he and I shared - I had never sat down with him and planned, for example, a calendar year's worth of events, six months' worth of storylines, or even a single show. That opportunity was equally as exciting to me.

From a financial perspective, it was an extremely lucrative opportunity. I left the meeting thinking to myself, 'This is going to be a great way to finish off my career in wrestling.'

On June 27th, 2019, WWE announced the shake-up in a press release that stunned the wrestling world:

Stamford, Conn. – WWE (NYSE: WWE) today announced that it has named Paul Heyman as Executive Director of *Monday Night Raw* and Eric Bischoff as Executive Director of *SmackDown Live*, newly created positions reporting directly to WWE Chairman & CEO Vince McMahon.

In their executive roles, Heyman and Bischoff will oversee the creative development of WWE's flagship programming and ensure integration across all platforms and lines of business. The creation of these roles further establishes WWE's ability to continuously reinvent its global brand while providing two distinct creative processes for its flagship shows.

Taking the job meant moving to Stamford, Connecticut – about as far removed from our life in Wyoming as you can get. But honestly: Loree and I knew that we'd be back. We basically said to each other, 'Okay – we've built a beautiful life in Wyoming over the last 20 years - we've got our home, our stuff...Nickie...and we're not gonna give everything up now.'

I mean, listen: I had worked my whole life to get to where I was, and particularly, to get to where we were living in Cody. It wasn't like I was going to put up the house and furniture for sale, move to Connecticut and leave all that behind permanently.

212

In my mind, I was going to give the position a *maximum* of three years, although honestly, I was kind of positioning for two years. I thought, 'If I can come in here, do a great job, get two years under my belt and really contribute…that's the way I want to end my career.' I didn't think I was going to be in WWE forever.

For now, though, Loree and I packed up the truck, got an eight-foot U Haul, took whatever we felt we needed to have with us, and started our drive across the country. It was literally like that sitcom from the '60's, the *Beverly Hillbillies* ("they loaded up the truck," goes the theme song to the show, "and they moved to Beverly…Hills, *that is.* Swimming pools and movie stars…")

On July 15th, I posted a clip of Loree and I driving on I-80, headed in the direction of New York City.

"Nope," I wrote alongside the clip. "Not in Wyoming anymore!"

I was about to start again in WWE – this time, as an executive – and I had barely asked any questions about the role. I had basically defaulted back to when I was 35 years old, thinking that I could adapt to any situation, without considering whether at 64, I might be less inclined to adapt.

In retrospect, there were a lot of questions I *should* have asked – and mostly questions of myself, by the way.

I didn't ask myself the following set of questions:

Are you sure you really want to do this?

213

Are you sure this is right for you, at this stage of your life?

Are you sure you're not just blindly jumping back into something that was a meaningful part of your life before?

Would I have asked myself those questions, I probably wouldn't have taken the job.

But I didn't.

And so I did (take the job, *that is*).

Third Grade Shit

18

I've often wondered what the impetus was for WWE to bring me back. Contrary to popular belief, I don't think it was Bruce saying, 'Hey, Vince – we need to get Eric,' nor do I think it was coming from Vince himself. What I do think – and what I know, quite frankly – is that WWE was in a period, to utilize an overused term, of 'reimagining' almost every aspect of their business.

Everybody recognized that the Fox deal was a major pivot point for WWE. I think there was an expectation that it was going to catapult the company to unprecedented levels of success, in terms of television ratings and all the things that come with that. As a result, WWE was stepping back and saying, 'Okay, we need to reexamine how we're approaching our business, because this additional responsibility – and the complexities involved in dealing with a new network – requires that we do things in a different way.'

In the entertainment industry, it's not uncommon for entities like WWE to undergo an auditing or evaluation process – to ensure that the creative output of the company, for example, is in alignment with the expectations of the audience, or is consistent with the evolution of the industry in general. In the case of WWE, its status as a publicly held company created additional expectations, relative to how its Board of Directors – and shareholders – viewed the operations of the company.

Through consultation with an external company, it was recommended that the creative process in WWE needed to be redesigned - hence the creation of 'Executive Director' roles, each with a direct report to Vince McMahon, for each of the primary shows. This would then free Vince up to focus on other things – whether that meant relaunching the XFL, the rebooted football league that he founded, or simply paying attention to other aspects of WWE.

This context (remember: *context is king*) was lost on the various 'reporters' who suggested – based on my experience working with network executives, I assume – that I had been hired as the 'middleman' between WWE and Fox. If one was to use guesswork, based on third-party information or hearsay, I can *kind* of see that making sense, but here's the truth: conversations between the two parties – WWE and Fox – were underway long before Eric Bischoff was hired as an executive.

It was not unheard of for decisions to be made, as a result of those conversations, that ultimately reached my ears much later. While I would 'check in' with the Fox executives – usually on a weekly basis, in order to resolve any open-ended issues – that was about it. Any suggestion that I was personally 'managing' the relationship between WWE and Fox is pure fiction.

I was hired to *oversee* anything that touched or related to *Smackdown* – including the creative process (although, in a key distinction, I wasn't brought in to create, *per se*. I was *managing* the process). That process, by the way, was unlike anything I was ever used to. Essentially, it would involve a series of meetings (the writers would develop the show all week long), leading to *another* meeting, this time with Vince, at "five o'clock" on Friday afternoons. None of the specific preparations for the show could occur before getting Vince's approval.

As I quickly learned, "five o'clock" on a Friday could soon turn into *midnight* on a Saturday morning, or two o'clock in the morning quite easily. We were often sitting around for six, seven or eight hours before Vince actually showed up. He would sit in his chair, look away and listen to the ideas, without ever once – in my time around him, at least – suggesting an idea of his own. When he heard something that he didn't like, a look of absolute disgust would come across his face. *Ugh!* he would yell with his head cocked back. *That's third...grade...shit!*

I don't relay this information to sound disrespectful to Vince, or towards WWE, by the way – the company has a market cap of five billion dollars, so clearly, they have experience in doing something right. But it was difficult, nonetheless – and certainly not the way in which creative, in my opinion, should have been structured.

We would wake up the next day (or the same day, more often than not) with everyone on standby, waiting for Vince to look at the revised draft. He might look at it during the morning, or maybe later in the afternoon, or perhaps at some point that night. He might want to get on the phone with a couple of people, or he might want to reconvene the entire group for a conference call. On the plane ride to the show, he might want to make more changes, and once the production meeting got underway – at the building, with hours to go before showtime – major elements of the show could shift yet again. On occasion, he might decide to start everything over *from scratch*.

Later in the afternoon, certain talent would then get access to Vince, and soon enough, the 'completed' show would be changing yet again. I was personally in the position, with two minutes to go before showtime, of waiting to get a last-minute change approved (ironic, considering I was often criticized for similar practices during my time in WCW). It takes a remarkable set of people to function in that environment – at the cost, I would argue, of the creative output itself.

It took a while to get settled into my new surroundings – a two-bedroom corporate apartment in downtown Stamford (coming from a 5000 square foot house on 20-plus acres of land – situated on the doorstep of Yellowstone National Park – it was a pretty big transition). Ironically, I now lived only a block-and-a-half away from Vince, and I would see him coming and going at all hours of the night.

At first, I enjoyed a little bit of a honeymoon period at WWE. Going in as an executive, I was mindful of the perception that arrived with me, and consequently, I focused on fitting in, learning the system, and *eventually* implementing my own vision for the show. I didn't want to be overly aggressive, especially in the creative arena, at the risk of giving ammunition to those who didn't want me there to begin with. You know, *There he goes – that's the Eric Bischoff we've heard about!*

After about six weeks in the job, however, I decided to assert myself a little more with Vince in the room. We were in another much-delayed creative meeting, at about one o'clock in the morning, when I started outlining a potential story - specifically relating to the re-introduction of a particular character. In doing so, I was coming from a completely different creative perspective, suggesting that we could turn the formula, so to speak, on its head just a little bit. I hadn't discussed the idea with anybody else on the team, but as I was just setting things up, I started noticing the reaction around me. There was one person in particular – someone who has been at WWE for a long time, back to when I was a talent – who looked at me with kind of a twinkle in his eye. There was a sense building as to where the idea was going.

I didn't even get far enough to actually present the idea, however, before Vince erupted in disgust.

Ugh!

That's horrible!

That's third...grade...shit!

Had I been 35 or 40 years old, I would have looked at Vince's reaction as a challenge. At 64, however, my mindset was different – I wasn't there to start a fight. I was in the position of Executive Director - or at least I thought I was - to *contribute*, and as a result, I wasn't going to fight someone over a particular idea. That's *not* collaboration, in my opinion - especially not the kind of collaboration that I was led to believe would be happening.

The reaction I received made me realize something: there was no fucking chance that this arrangement was going to work. This was not *re-imagining the process* – you know, the beautiful vision that was presented to me before I agreed to the job. This was the exact fucking opposite.

As the meeting continued, I discreetly pulled off my company ID, grabbed the corporate phone from out of my pocket, and placed both on the table in front of me. I was within a minute of getting up and saying, 'I'm out of here.'

It was past two o'clock in the morning before the meeting actually ended. When I got in my car to drive home, the adrenaline was flowing at levels I hadn't experienced in a long time. I knew I couldn't sleep thinking about the exchange, so I got out of the $2200 suit I had been wearing for 18 hours (that's another thing: wearing a fucking suit every day to a creative job is *ridiculous*) and put on a pair of sweats instead. I grabbed Nickie and took her for a walk outside my apartment building.

As we sat down on a nearby bench, I looked up at Vince's condo building. I knew he was up there, and like clockwork, the lights went on in his penthouse apartment. I thought about something he had said when I first came back: *You can call me 24/7, pal – you need me, you call me!*

Typically, Vince was very good at getting back to me (he was also good at calling in the middle of the night – unannounced - wanting to discuss the intricacies of a show). It was clear that we needed to talk – now more than ever – and knowing myself, I knew that if I didn't get the feeling off my chest, it was only going to get worse.

I called his cell – no answer.

I sent him a text – *Vince, I really need to talk to you.*

No answer.

The lights were on – I knew Vince was there – but I didn't get a response.

I eventually let it go, talking myself out of raising the issue with Vince again.

But it was telling, I thought - I never did get that response.

The Honeymoon's Over, Honey

19

By now, my optimism towards the new job was rapidly waning. I found myself telling Loree a variation of the same thing each day: *keep as much of our stuff in boxes as you can.*

I was starting to see how the WWE *process* (and, by proxy, the company culture created around that process) existed in direct opposition to what I was used to. Prior to my hiring as Executive Director, I had essentially operated as a one-man band – by virtue of being self-employed for 20 years - as opposed to leading an orchestra, if you will, and having a staff of people reporting to me.

In retrospect, that transition was one that I *overestimated* my ability to adapt to. After all, I had been living in Cody, Wyoming – surrounded by beautiful mountains in the middle of nowhere – enjoying complete control over my schedule. While I had done the corporate thing before, I didn't realize what a change it would be at 64 years old – waiting around in that creative room, sweating in that $2200 suit, not knowing what time I was going to be home.

Sensing my own difficulty to adapt, I wondered if I could persist in the role for as long as the timeframe I had targeted earlier – two years, give or take. It was *never* a consideration of mine that it might end sooner:

Stamford, Conn., October 15, 2019 – WWE (NYSE: WWE) today announced that it has named Bruce Prichard the Executive Director of Friday Night SmackDown, reporting directly to WWE Chairman & CEO Vince McMahon. Prichard will oversee the creative development of Friday Night SmackDown on FOX and ensure integration across all platforms and lines of business, replacing Eric Bischoff.

Let's back up for a minute. On October 4th, 2019, the much-touted debut of *Smackdown* on Fox attracted an audience of 3.9 million viewers – peaking at about 4.2 million viewers for the appearance of Dwayne 'The Rock' Johnson.

If you understand the television business, you know that the season premiere of *anything* tends to rate about 25-30 percent higher than the rest of the season. In the case of *Smackdown*, the follow-up edition of the show – airing on October 11th, 2019 – generated an audience consistent with that rule (2.9 million viewers tuned in - representing a 25% drop from week one).

In other words, the decrease in viewers (3.9 million to 2.9 million) observed after the first Fox show falls right in line with the traditional deterioration that one would expect after a show's premiere (for some perspective, the *highest* rated episode of Smackdown in 2022 – as of the time of this writing – attracted an average of *2.5 million* viewers). Nonetheless, the dirtsheets ran with the obvious narrative: Eric Bischoff's firing owed itself to the "disastrous" drop in ratings from week one to week two (an alternative version of the narrative posited that WWE, apparently in anticipation of Fox's discontent with the ratings, had hired me purposefully to be an eventual scapegoat).

As per usual, their 'reporting' emanated from a place of total ignorance. If my performance was based on the ratings coming out of *two shows*, I don't think Steven Spielberg would have lasted any longer than I did. It might make logical sense for an *outsider* to connect those dots, but my firing had *nothing* to do with ratings – and everything to do with my inability to adapt.

As a result of that inability to adapt, Vince decided that I wasn't the right person for the role. It was more of a chemistry issue than anything else, but ultimately, I have to take responsibility for it.

I didn't live up to the job.

If you want to know the truth, here's where I really fucked up. I went into WWE with too much apprehension related to how I would be *perceived* – based on the pre-existing narrative that I had been 'difficult to work with' in the past. That reputation was always blown out of proportion, but it affected my ability to implement the ideas that I thought would help the product. As noted earlier, my strategy was to 'fit in' to the WWE system and not be too aggressive at the outset.

I don't think that's what Vince was looking for.

Vince wants to be surrounded by aggressive people – people like him, essentially – or people who operate in a manner consistent with his approach. He wants people to take control of a situation, or better yet, to take *ownership* over what they're doing. While it certainly would have been easy, from day one really, for me to portray myself as an *alpha* executive – it's not alien to my nature – I saw it having the potential to rub others the wrong way. Looking back on it now, that may have been a miscalculation.

When the decision finally came down, I found myself feeling more *relieved* – albeit surprised – as opposed to anything else (I also took the jokes that I had lasted *83 Days* in good fun – Conrad and I sold a T-shirt with that phrase. For the record, it was *110 Days* – but who's counting?).

Once the day arrived, it actually wasn't Vince who delivered the news to me (he was in Saudi Arabia at the time, making preparations for WWE's *Crown Jewel* pay-per-view event). It was just a typical Tuesday morning at first: I showed up to the office at around 9:30am (most of the writers – many of whom would take trains in from New York City, typically arrived about an hour later), but as I was getting prepared for the day, a couple of things seemed off.

First, I caught eyes with the person who ultimately would let me go. As he entered his office, he seemed more hurried than usual – only quickly looking over in my direction – and then I looked over at my secretary, whose eyes immediately diverted downward. Just seconds earlier, she appeared to have been in deep conversation with Vince's assistant.

Okay…that's weird, I thought to myself.

It wasn't clicking yet – maybe I hadn't had enough caffeine at that point – even as I found myself in a room with HR.

There must be an issue with someone on the writing team, I figured.

As soon as the HR rep started talking, however, I came to a different realization.

Oh, this is about me!

Now, like anyone else, I've heard stories regarding the termination process and how it is often handled in a corporate environment: the sight of someone being escorted out of the building - as if they had just been caught shoplifting - *that* type of thing.

In my case, however, the termination process was anything but typical. Although I *was* required to turn in my corporate phone and laptop – as one would obviously expect - I was *also* given the chance to address my team on the way out. I've seen other people get fired in WWE before, and they certainly didn't get that opportunity.

I walked into a conference room where the unsuspecting writers were waiting for me. *This is my last day,* I said – getting straight to the point. *I want you guys to know that I really enjoyed working with you. Each one of you, individually, are incredible people. Collectively, this is an amazing team, and you guys work for an amazing company. Keep it up – enjoy this moment – and make the most of this opportunity.*

It's unlike anything else that you'll ever experience again.

Some people at WWE believed that Vince should have been there when I was fired. Personally, I was fine with it – my feelings weren't hurt or anything, and I didn't feel disrespected in any way, shape or form. Again, my overwhelming feeling was that of *relief*; so much so, in fact, that the person firing me seemed more upset than I was!

For about a month after the news was made public, Bruce Prichard would check in with me on occasion, trying his best to give the situation some closure:

Hey, Eric - have you heard from Vince yet?

No, I haven't, Bruce - but it's no big deal, I responded.

Vince doesn't have to call me – I don't care.

Everything's great.

No, no, Bruce would say. *Vince needs to call you!*

Finally - from what I understand - Bruce went to Vince and asked him directly.

Uh, Vince - why in the hell aren't you calling Eric?

I've been calling him! replied Vince.

I've been leaving him messages, he continued, *but Eric won't call me back!*

By now, Bruce was really perplexed.

What number are you calling Eric on?

Vince turned to Bruce and showed him the number.

Bruce now realized where our wires had got crossed.

Vince! That's his corporate phone! He turned it in when you fired him!

A day later, Vince called me on my personal cell phone, and we found ourselves agreeing on two points in particular.

First: time affects people in different ways.

Second: it just wasn't the right time for me to come back.

During my time at WWE, All Elite Wrestling (AEW) made its debut on TNT, marking the return of professional wrestling on the Turner networks.

From the outset, I was somewhat skeptical about AEW, most notably due to a) the state of the television industry - circa 2019, and b) the fact that WWE was such a dominant player in the industry. Previously, my impression had been that most cable outlets either *had* wrestling (i.e. USA Network), had previously tried it and weren't interested any longer, or simply viewed wrestling as an unattractive *niche* product.

In large part, that set of assumptions was based on conversations that I had engaged in – *while I was still active in the television business* – with networks, studios and various TV executives. To that end, my skepticism had nothing to do with Tony Khan - the founder of AEW and son of billionaire businessman Shahid Khan - or anything to do with the Khan family in general. At first, I didn't even know who the Khan family was, nor did I know what kind of resources they had at their disposal.

With that in mind, I was pretty surprised at the announcement that AEW was coming to TNT. On the other hand, given the involvement of Kevin Reilly (the executive with whom I had met in 2001 – as mentioned earlier in Chapter 4), I knew that AEW would be interfacing with someone possessing a pretty good idea about professional wrestling – including how successful it had been in the past. *Maybe this could actually work*, I thought to myself at the time.

I actually watched the first episode of *AEW Dynamite* from an interesting vantage point – the writer's room at WWE headquarters. We were pulling an all-nighter – as established, that wasn't unusual by any means – and I came away saying, '*Hmmm*. I'll be damned. This is kind of interesting.'

From my perspective, the production quality of AEW was the aspect of its presentation that stood out the most. It was a little gritty – a little rough around the edges – which is precisely how I think wrestling should be presented. Surrounded by a bunch of WWE writers and others who were part of the team, I shared the fact that I already liked AEW's production *more* than the production of NXT (WWE decided to pit NXT, its developmental brand, in opposition to AEW on Wednesday nights).

While I received a few odd looks upon making that observation – relative to AEW's production quality and presentation – I was intrigued to see how things would develop. After leaving WWE, I dropped in on the AEW product periodically, and overall, I was *fairly* impressed. It was clear that as a new company, AEW was experiencing some growing pains, but before long, the shows started to improve (as of the time of this writing, however, AEW has failed to exceed the audience for its first-ever show – 1.4 million viewers on average).

At some point in the summer of 2020, Cody Rhodes reached out to me with a message. *Chris Jericho has an idea,* Cody told me, *and he'd really like to work you into this segment – if you're up for it.*

Sure, I replied, *why not?*

I ended up guesting on the August 5th, 2020 edition of *Dynamite* – my first appearance on TNT in 20 years. I had a blast doing it – the 'new car smell', if you will, still existed with AEW – and my impression of the backstage environment was very positive. People were *having fun,* and I saw more laughing and joking than I had seen in many years (a couple of months later, I made another cameo on *Dynamite,* returning twice still in early 2021).

In October 2021, Tony Khan then came out with some puzzling comments regarding Ted Turner, as posted on his Twitter page:

I've never met Ted Turner. It's very possible Ted Turner is smarter than me, but he didn't know 1% of what I know about professional wrestling or WCW would still be on TNT/TBS.

Those comments just *lit me up*. Number one, Tony's show – in case he had forgotten – aired on TNT, which stands for *Turner Network Television*. It was therefore disrespectful to make those comments in reference to Ted. Secondly, the comments were just stupid, reflecting – and I mean this in the most literal sense – *ignorance* (as in, lack of information or knowledge).

Tony Khan has no idea about what happened in WCW – he only knows what he's heard from dirtsheet writers and people on the periphery of the business (who themselves don't have any idea). It wasn't until in 2018 - when the book *Nitro: The Incredible Rise and Inevitable Collapse of Ted Turner's WCW* was published – that anybody ever attempted to address what happened behind the scenes in Turner Broadcasting *as a whole*.

Look, I'm loyal to a fault. If you disrespect someone who I hold in high regard – or a close friend or family member – I'm probably more defensive in those situations than I am when someone attacks *me*.

Consequently, I responded with some comments of my own which aired on *83 Weeks*:

If Tony were to call me and ask for any advice, here's what it would be — shut up and wrestle, dude.

Just put out the best product you can and you've proven you can. Focus on that. Now this is weird coming from me, right? The guy who challenged Vince McMahon. The guy who gave away their finishes. But here's the difference. I was actually competing with him. I was going head-to-head. Real head-to-head. Like, my show started the same time his show started each and every week.

For the record, I wasn't advocating for AEW to engage in head-to-head competition with WWE – they would get crushed.

Nonetheless, Tony was spending so much time – and still does, to this day – creating the *illusion* that AEW is a competitor to WWE. In fairness, I have *heard* – although perhaps this is an excuse – that for AEW, going head-to-head against WWE (on Monday Nights, at least) would mean going head-to-head against *Monday Night Football* (and thus creating a conflict of interest for the Khan family, who also own the Jacksonville Jaguars).

In any event, if you're not going to get in the ring – so to speak – and actually prove what you're saying, you shouldn't mouth off from the sidelines.

Especially if you're going to disrespect Ted Turner – a true pioneer in the business that you are hoping to have success in.

I continued:

...And another thing, Tony comes out and says, 'We're at the 1996 stage of WCW and we're going to not make their mistakes.' Tony, you're inventing some mistakes, brother. By coming out there and constantly comparing yourself or deriding your competition, but not having the willingness — I almost said *balls* — the willingness to say, 'Okay, let's go head-to-head. Let's really compete. Let's see who can get whose market share.' That's real competition. So, I'm a little disappointed in the rhetoric that I'm hearing out of Tony, as well as some of the talent. Man, shut the fuck up. Until you're actually competing and you're actually competing favorably — and by the way, Tony, in 1996 I was kicking WWE's ass. Every week! In a real head-to-head competition, not a cosplay competition.

In response to my own comments, Tony went *nuts*. A very close friend of mine relayed that he had been receiving text messages from

Tony – on the subject of what I said – throughout an entire afternoon. I was driving in my truck – coming home with Loree after visiting family in Minneapolis – when this friend of mine called me.

Hey man, can you give Tony a call?

He's been blowing my phone up all day – he just can't believe you said what you said.

Alright, I responded. *I'll call Tony – I'll put a Band-Aid on this.*

No big deal – maybe I could have said things a little nicer.

I left Tony a very nice message. *Hey, Tony,* I essentially said, *I'm on the road right now, but I understand that you're upset. Let's talk about it – just give me a shout at your convenience.*

I let my friend know that I had left the message. *Yeah,* he responded, *Tony texted me and said he's busy right now – he's in meetings - but he's gonna get back to you.*

Tony never did get back to me.

That's a little chickenshit, in my opinion. It wasn't like Tony *owed* me that call, but if he was willing to contact somebody who I knew – in order to let me know he was upset in the first place – why not just pick up the phone and call me (even if it was just a short, 'Fuck You,' kind of conversation)?

To this day, Tony continues to occasionally reference WCW – typically some variation of 'AEW is never gonna make the same mistakes that WCW did.'

Well, guess what? If you look at what has transpired in 2022, Tony has not only made more mistakes than WCW, he's made mistakes that I never *thought* of making.

Part of me is tempted to say, 'That's wrestling karma 101 for you.' The other part of me still wants AEW to succeed – mostly because I want the wrestling business to succeed.

Let me be clear: I have no desire to be in the wrestling business again personally. As always, *Never Say Never*, but the odds are pretty frickin' slim that I'd ever get involved in the business again – and I'm cool with that.

For the first time, I actually feel safe to say the following: *wrestling is firmly in my rear-view mirror.*

I still want the business to do well, and I still hope that AEW can evolve beyond making so many fundamental mistakes, which – in my view – have now gone far beyond growing pains. If Tony doesn't make it, it's gonna be a long time before anybody else gets a shot.

With that being said, he *never* should have disrespected Ted.

SCAN ME

Full Circle

20

I could almost set my watch to it.

At a certain point each January, coinciding - not so coincidentally - with the onset of *Wrestlemania* season, the inevitable chatter would commence: will Bischoff 'get in' this year?

My social media would blow up. I would go through countless fan messages on the subject. To participate in an interview meant a familiar set of questions:

Say, Eric, how do you feel about 'getting in?'

Will it bother you if you don't get recognized?

If you did make it in, who would you want to induct you?

If you had that opportunity - theoretically, of course - what would you like to say?

...and what does it really mean to you, anyway?

The speculation, of course, concerned the *WWE Hall of Fame*, an annual ceremony that confers the highest level of status in our business. From 2004 onwards, the ceremony has been tethered to *Wrestlemania* itself, ensuring a lively spectacle for fans on the day prior to the big event. I had some experience with the festivities myself - first as an attendee, and then, in 2017, as an honorary speaker for DDP.

Over time, I kind of became numb to it - the gossip and the talk (or the *rumor and innuendo* - to coin a phrase). When someone asked me about it – the notion that Eric Bischoff may be inducted in the WWE Hall of Fame - my response was pretty much the same: *if it happens, it happens.*

Outwardly, I was ambivalent about it all, but part of that was me being defensive. *Protective* might be a better word – because truthfully, I didn't want to be disappointed.

In a public forum, I didn't want to consider talking about something that seemed far from an actual reality - but deep down, it certainly bothered me.

It would be disingenuous to suggest otherwise. We all want to be recognized, especially by our peers, for our contributions in whatever we do. I think that's just human nature, and just like anyone else, I imagined myself enjoying the experience immensely.

At the same time, I had no control over whether or not WWE inducted me, and as I've learned - sometimes the hard way - it's best not to be affected by things you can't control.

By the time 2020 began, the subject had comfortably become something that I didn't much think about. I guess I didn't *allow* it to bother me.

But then - all of a sudden - it *did* become a reality.

When I finally got *that* phone call, the feeling was overwhelming. In that moment, I was hit with a real sense of accomplishment, maybe owing to the fact that above all, the most significant part of my career had been *outside* of WWE.

During that time, the intensity of our competition was real - that much is well documented. It was emotional, it was trying, and it was...*raw*, for lack of a better word. I was going after Vince on a very personal level - challenging him to a fight on pay-per-view, at one point. To wrestling fans, that might seem kind of silly, or ridiculous in hindsight, but let me tell you - that was a *personal affront* to Vince McMahon. If I hadn't been careful - maybe if I was walking across the street somewhere in downtown Stamford back then - I'm not so sure he wouldn't have tried to run me over.

When I went to work with WWE as a talent, nobody thought I would last very long - let alone three-and-a-half years. Then again, my tenure as an executive - albeit many years later - had been for a period of only four months. Nonetheless, here I was presented with an opportunity to come *full circle* - to bookend my association with WWE at the very highest level.

Another thought soon hit me. When the day arrived, I soon realized, the once-hated Eric Bischoff would be standing there – moments before hitting the stage – next to Vince McMahon himself.

Prior to my induction in 2021, the founding members of the nWo (Hulk, Kevin Nash and Scott Hall) were announced as inductees in 2020. At the time, WWE was *really* putting pressure on me to be there – they wanted me sitting in the audience specifically – although the event was ultimately canceled due to the COVID-19 pandemic. Mark Carrano (WWE's then-Head of Talent Relations) was the first to approach me about it.

Although it was January 2020 when Carrano called – three months after WWE had terminated my contract – Loree and I were still not back in Wyoming. Rather than rush home, we had decided to take our time, decompress a little bit, and slowly move out of my corporate apartment in Stamford (incidentally, the apartment had six months remaining on the lease anyway). With the holidays on the horizon, we then headed down to the Tampa area for about six weeks, eventually starting our long drive home after the New Year.

We stopped in Rockford, Illinois one night when Carrano ultimately reached out. *Hey, Eric,* he said, *we would really love to have you at Wrestlemania this year. It's in Tampa, and we were really hoping that you would be in the audience for the Hall of Fame ceremony.*

It was somewhat ironic that Loree and I had just *left* Tampa, but more importantly, we hadn't been home (Wyoming) for almost six months. *Hey, Mark,* I replied. *I really, really appreciate it...but I can't do it, man. I gotta get home – I gotta get my life back together again and pick up where I left off.*

The Chairman really wants you to be there, Mark said.

I'm sure he does, I replied, *but I can't do it. I physically can't be there.*

Later that night, Bruce Prichard called me about the exact same subject.

Eric, I just talked to Mark, and he told me why you can't be there. I get all that – but Vince would really like you to be there.

I know, I responded, *Mark told me that. I appreciate that...and it means a lot to me that we still have enough of a relationship where he wants me to be there. But I can't do it.*

Eric, Bruce said, unrelentingly. *I'm asking you this as a favor – would you please come to Wrestlemania?*

That's weird, I thought to myself. *Why would that be a favor?*

It still didn't make sense to me, but Bruce knew one thing - if a close friend of mine asks me for a *favor*, I don't really need to hear anything else. In that situation – if it's within my power - I'm typically going to do it.

Alright, Bruce, I sighed. *I'll be there.*

Unbeknownst to me, the reason that WWE wanted me in the audience for the nWo's induction (i.e. during the unfortunately canceled 2020 ceremony) was because they had a plan – a plan to surprise *me* (the king of surprises, after all!) with my own Hall of Fame induction.

I only found out after the ceremony was canceled - and once I started getting calls from Hulk and Kevin Nash. *Hey, bro,* Hulk said in one conversation, *just so you know – we were gonna smarten you up beforehand.*

We wouldn't want you to get blindsided.

For the record, I wouldn't have minded getting blindsided!

WWE had it all laid out – and it certainly would have been a very cool moment.

A year later, Carrano called me again.

Eric, I gotta tell you something. We really want to induct you into the Hall of Fame – by yourself.

And just so you know, here's what was supposed to happen last year...

(I didn't let Mark know that I already knew – I wasn't going to breach that level of confidentiality with Hulk and Kevin.)

It wasn't until March 18th, 2021 – when I was invited to appear on WWE's *After the Bell* podcast - that the news was made public. Corey Graves delivered some heartfelt words as he made the announcement:

Eric, after all these years and contributions you have made to the sports entertainment industry...it is our honor and our pleasure to inform you that you, Eric Bischoff, will be inducted as a member of the 2021 class of the WWE Hall of Fame. Congratulations.

Even though I already knew (as did my wife and my children – but that was about it), I got really emotional after hearing Corey's announcement. Viewers watched me struggle to deliver a coherent response as I got choked up with tears:

Wow...thank you. I don't...I don't know quite what to say.

...Just...wow. That's all I got.

For a guy who could never shut the hell up on my own podcast, I don't have anything to say.

It was finally now out there – it was finally now *real*.

I approached my Hall of Fame speech in a manner similar to everything I ever did on camera. I didn't think about it too much, and consequently, it basically came from my heart. Generally speaking, I knew how I felt – relative to my career and the things that were most important to me – and I was determined to make it as positive as possible.

When it was almost time to go out, Vince pulled me aside.

He said something in a very private manner to me – something that I'm almost hesitant to reveal here.

Eric, he said, *I just want you to know that you turned this business upside down. You changed this business in a way that nobody else has.*

Vince's words were heartfelt – I could feel it. It was the most genuine, sincere conversation that I ever had with him. To then walk through the curtain – to feel the intensity of that *full circle* moment – it was all very, very emotional for me:

Wow – thank you so much. This…this is amazing. It truly is.

…You know, little did I know – 34 years ago – when I jumped in my car and headed over to Verne Gagne's office in the AWA in Minneapolis…that I was about to embark on a life-long road trip.

The first leg of that journey, in Minneapolis, [allowed] me to learn the fundamentals of a business that – to that point – I only got to experience from a distance. As a fan.

…Eventually, it was time to say goodbye. That road trip was over – and it was time to start a new one.

So I jumped in my car and headed to Atlanta – for an amazing opportunity that would change my life forever…and the lives of my family. An opportunity that would give me the freedom to explore the 'What if's' in my imagination. But like any great road trip, it came to an end.

Or so I thought – until one summer morning, I was in the office when my phone rang, and I got invited to go on *another* journey. This one more improbable…not improbable…I thought it was absolutely *impossible*…but it was a journey that provided me with invaluable opportunities – and most importantly, experience.

What have I learned along the way? *Nanos gigantum humeris insidentes*. It's a latin phrase, and it comes from Greek mythology. It roughly translates to *standing on the shoulders of giants.*

I've realized that all of the amazing things that I've gotten to do – including standing here in this moment – this amazing road trip that I've been on is because I've had the privilege of standing on the shoulders of the giants that came before me.

And as I stand here right now, on this amazing platform – one of the most successful platforms in the world of entertainment – I wanna thank the giants that gave me that opportunity.

And those giants are the people that have taken this industry we love – from what was once a traveling circus, or a sideshow as a part of the traveling circus – to become one of the most powerful forms of entertainment, anywhere in the world.

This is a uniquely *American* art form – and it's those giants that we have to give thanks to.

And I want to thank each and every one of you people – I say that sincerely. I want to thank each and every one of you people, from the bottom of my heart. No matter where you are in the universe, thank you for being a part of this road trip – this journey. Thank you for joining me.

I've been asked if the Hall of Fame experience was the 'crowning achievement' of my career. That's certainly one way of looking at it – but do me a favor. Go back and listen to the last sentence I said in my speech:

It's been one hell of a ride…and the best is *still to come.*

That last sentence was spontaneous – it wasn't something that I thought about in advance. It just kind of *happened.*

I'm not a psychiatrist, but maybe it was my subconscious speaking, as if to let the world know that I wasn't going anywhere. In my mind, I was probably fighting the notion that the Hall of Fame was going to be my swan song, or some kind of video headstone.

More than anything else, however, I simply felt *grateful.*

On July 22nd, 2022, Vince abruptly announced his retirement – for reasons that I won't explore here – via a short message on Twitter:

At 77, time for me to retire. Thank you, WWE Universe. Then. Now. Forever. Together.

I'm not quite sure how I feel about Vince's retirement, other than feeling some sense of disappointment. It's mind-boggling to think about how much Vince changed the industry – and to consider how he built WWE into such a global media and cultural phenomenon. For Vince to have achieved so much in the industry – beyond what anybody else, in their wildest dreams, ever thought possible – it's regrettable that his legacy has now been tainted.

While we're not close, I like to consider myself a friend to Vince, and I look forward to seeing him – whenever I do. Despite everything that we've been through, our relationship is still cordial, and I enjoy exchanging a text or two with him during the holidays. In any event – regardless of if we were on good terms or not - to see

Vince McMahon end his career on such a sour note…well, again, it's *disappointing*.

He's such a complex character. A number of news outlets have reached out to me about the Vince McMahon 'story' – including a television network that recently did a special entitled *The Nine Lives of Vince McMahon* – in hopes that I would talk to them about the subject.

I didn't want anything to do with it.

I think there's gonna be a lot of people that will exploit an already negative situation – simply in order to create some revenue from it. I just don't want to be a part of anything like that – out of respect, I guess, more than anything else.

When I think about Vince's family – particularly his grandchildren – I hope that they haven't been too affected by the situation. In my own experience around Vince, I saw for myself that he loves his family *dearly*.

One thing is for sure: they'll *never* be another person like Vince McMahon.

...*Still To Come*

21

It's one thing to achieve success, but another to achieve it, lose it, and achieve it again. Upon filing for bankruptcy, you might recall that I was given *six* years to repay my debts – substantial as they were at that time.

Well, I did it in *three*.

So have I made a complete comeback?

Not quite – but close.

I'm not going to lie - that makes me feel good.

On September 10th, 1999 – the day when I was 'sent home' from my position at WCW - I believed that my time in professional wrestling was over. It looked that way again in 2000, and then again in 2001, when WWE purchased what was left of WCW as a company. *For sure*, I thought that the expiration of my WWE contract, in 2007, meant that wrestling was firmly in my *rear-view mirror* – until I found myself, most unintendedly, getting involved with TNA in 2009.

Even *more* unlikely was my return to WWE, this time as an executive, in 2019 – ten years after my TNA chapter began.

Everything about that journey is very, very unlikely – including WWE deciding to induct *me* (the once-hated Eric Bischoff!) into their Hall of Fame in 2021.

What were the odds of all that happening?

Pretty slim.

But I'm grateful for it – especially when I consider starting my own production company, and the success that Jason and I had for a period of 10 or 12 years. It was immensely gratifying to find that success, it really was - especially as an independent television producer, operating *outside* of professional wrestling. That was a pretty unlikely achievement, too.

All of it, truly – inside and outside of wrestling – has been bonus points since day one.

As of late 2022, I'm still a fairly divisive character in the world of wrestling. I'm outspoken - I still have strong opinions – and I'm never afraid to express those opinions. That can add up to a fairly polarizing perception - especially in today's environment.

There are those who have a pretty thorough understanding of the impact that WCW - and especially *Nitro* - had on the wrestling industry in the 1990's (and especially its influence on the style, format and presentation of wrestling today). That portion of the audience tends to be pretty open-minded and knowledgeable, but then you have a portion of the audience that is the exact opposite – the Internet wrestling community, Reddit, dirt sheet kind of universe. A lot of people in *that* community will hold on to certain narratives about me, my time running WCW, or any number of things they've read online. Those opinions, uninformed as they are, are often fairly negative.

In general, though, the reaction that I get - especially when I make public appearances these days – tends to be much more honest than anything you're going to read online. Generally speaking, I think there's a real appreciation for what WCW did, what it meant to people, and how it either introduced – or brought back – many fans to pro wrestling. It's all very positive, and honestly, I think that my reputation has probably been enhanced greatly over time.

Time has a tendency to do that. Time has a tendency to put things in perspective, whereas a current observation may not. I often think that those favorable reactions - when I do get them – probably have a lot more to do with *time* than anything else.

It's funny. I can remember being a young kid, and my teachers would consistently write the same thing on my report card: *no focus.* Or it would be some variation of the following: *he's very smart, but he just won't pay attention. He won't stay focused.*

Looking back, I realize now that my "lack of focus" was really a result of being intellectually curious. I'm interested in so many different things, and sometimes it's hard for me to stay focused on something, especially if it fails to capture my imagination. When something *does* capture my imagination, on the other hand - and particularly if there's a chance to learn something new – well *now* you've got my attention.

The way I see it, when you fail to embrace an opportunity to learn something new, or simply quit having an open mind about such opportunities, that's when you're starting to get old. I don't care if you're in your thirties or your forties, if you get to the point where you wake up and say, 'This is my life. This is who I am, and this is what my life's gonna be'…that's when you start dying, in my opinion.

For me, I think I'm gonna work 'til the day I die - or until there's a point where it's physically impossible for me to contribute something. I *cringe* when I hear people talk about how much they're looking forward to retirement. I've simply seen too many people – my father was one of them – who worked their entire lives, did 'everything right', put up with shit they never should have put up with…all with the ultimate goal to *retire*.

Well, in my father's case, he did retire…and then he died.

When *my* time comes, I know a few things for certain.

Firstly, for my family, I don't want it to be any more painful than it has to be.

Secondly, I want to make sure that I can help my family long after I'm gone. I want to make sure that my kids are well taken care of, and I didn't always think *like that*. Quite frankly, I've always been able to make money, but because of some of the risks I took – the beer business and online gaming projects among them – I burned up a lot of that money, a lot of the money that I could have left to my children.

Thankfully, I'm well on my way to rebuilding what I had to leave them.

I want to make sure that I've said everything that I really wanted to say, and so I do that, each and every day, with respect to the people that I love and hold closely. I don't want to be going 'out the door' thinking, 'God, I wish I would've said this or that to this person…'

Speaking of which, I also want to make sure that I'm right with God.

I'm doing all of these things right now, making sure that when the time comes, all of my boxes have been checked.

As I look back on my life, I try to think about the lessons I've learned along the way – and what other people can take from my experiences.

One of the major lessons I've learned relates to controlling one's emotions – or, more specifically, not allowing others to control your emotional state.

Consider the following story: the year is 1977. I'm about 22 years old and I'm on my Harley, enjoying a cruise on a Saturday afternoon. As I wait at a four-way stop, a car rolls into the intersection – we're on a gravel road, mind you – before the driver performs a series of 'donuts' on the road.

By design, apparently, his maneuver spits rocks and gravel *all over me.*

Nah, I think to myself, *that doesn't work.*

The car takes off – I notice there's two guys in the vehicle – but I take off after them. I chase 'em for 10 miles, then 20 – then 30 – and

247

eventually, we get neck-and-neck on the highway. We're going about 60 miles per hour now, and in a fit of rage, I pull up right next to these sons-of-bitches.

Before you know it, I'm *stomping* on the side of their car – yelling at the top of my lungs - demanding that they pull over!

By the time they finally *do* pull in somewhere, I've been chasing these guys for 45 minutes. I'm not quite as fired up anymore, and besides, it looks like these guys are teenagers anyway. They're apologetic as we meet face to face.

Ah - I'll let this one slide.

I think about that story now and shake my head. What they did was disrespectful, sure – and potentially dangerous – but it was really no big deal. I mean, think about it: I'm flying down the highway in a Harley – trying to kick the door in on two teenage kids who just did something stupid.

I could have been *killed* that day – *over absolutely nothing.*

Had that incident gone another way, you never would have heard from Eric Bischoff – nor would you be reading these words that I'm writing right now.

If people cut me off today, I don't 'motherfuck' them.

I wave to 'em now.

I love my life today.

248

Recently, Loree and I were in Florida together, visiting with our kids and our new grandson – Waylon James Bischoff (affectionately known as 'WayJay' for short). It was a Saturday night, and we decided to go out and grab a drink - just the two of us - before finding ourselves at a beautiful restaurant, right on the beach.

As we sat down at the corner of the bar, a group of three ladies came over to join us. One of them was dressed, quite noticeably to Loree and I, *to the nines* – I mean, you could tell that she had spent the entire day getting ready to go out. She was there with her daughter and her daughter-in-law, and let me tell you, they were all having a blast.

At one point, the well-dressed lady was having a hard time getting her sweater off, and naturally, I reached over to give her some help. This got us chatting a little bit, and before long, I found out something interesting about her.

She was 93 years old!

93!

Naturally, we started chatting a little bit more, and as we did, Loree and I found the lady so interesting, so outgoing...so friendly and conversational.

Before she got up and left that night, she left us with some parting words.

I learned something a long time ago, she told us.

The minute you stop using your mind is the minute you start getting old.

Well, I've made up my mind, she said.

I'm never gonna get old!

We cracked up and smiled listening to her - so much so, in fact, that we all made plans to catch up again in the future. It was just so refreshing, really, because so often among my peers – and across society as a whole – I hear the exact opposite sentiment. In the entertainment industry, for example, you encounter a lot of people that believe – although they keep this closely guarded – that the best part of their lives was in the past.

That's not unique to the entertainment business, either. How many times do we hear people say, 'Oh man, when I was in high school…' – I'll never understand getting nostalgic for high school, by the way – or 'College – the best years of my life…'

My perspective, for what it's worth, is that any period in *the past* should never be viewed as the 'best part' of your life. You just shouldn't say that to yourself, in my opinion. I know that personally, I'm determined to never fall into that trap, and it *is* a trap – as I see it.

I wouldn't trade my life today for *anything*. I guess if I wanted to live in the past, I could walk around and pretend that it's 1997 for the rest of my life. That was probably the peak of my success, on an individual level, and certainly the peak of WCW's success as a company. At that time, it was as if we could do no wrong.

But to go *back* to 1997? Ugh. I'll simply never - under any circumstances – look back and think that *any time* in the past was 'the best part' of my life.

The best is *always* still to come, and I approach every day accordingly.

Like everyone else, I've had my share of ups and downs. I think about times when my biggest problem was figuring out, along with an accountant, how not to pay as much in taxes as it looked like I should be paying. Then there were times in which I asked, 'How am I gonna keep this thing afloat?'

In the beginning, my journey in professional wrestling was ignited by a sense of adventure, and a willingness to take risks. But what really got me *through it* – especially to the point where I'm at today - is having a sense of gratitude. If there's anything that I hope readers will take away from this book, it's how much I've learned about the power of being grateful.

Look, I don't know about anybody else. I'm not preaching up here – *trust* me on that one - and I certainly don't claim to be an expert on motivating others. I can only share what has worked for me - and how best I've been able to motivate myself.

I try to wake up each morning and be grateful for my health, for my family and their wellbeing, and for the opportunities that may arise on any given day. I try to acknowledge some of the simpler things that are in front of me every day, while recognizing the things that bring me closer to God. In turn – and in my experience - that makes me feel even more grateful, which makes me feel more positive, and ultimately, more confident in whatever I'm trying to do.

I just wouldn't know *how* to get up every morning and attack new projects, new ideas, and new moments in life if I wasn't grateful for the things I have around me every day. I don't think I could be positive enough to have any hope of being successful.

Ultimately, I think that out of all the things I have learned along the way, the most valuable has been learning to appreciate what I have.

Not what I used to have, by the way – and certainly not what I don't have.

But being grateful for what I *do* have, which in health, family, and perspective – not to mention Nickie here by my side – is a helluva lot, *mucker futhers*.

Gratitude is what keeps me going.

Gratitude, like context, is king.

Acknowledgments

Trying to prepare the *Acknowledgments* section was a real challenge for me – mostly because there are so many people that deserve to be acknowledged!

Obviously, my wife, Loree and my children – Garett and Montanna – are the most important people in the world to me.

I want to talk a little bit about Montanna. Many wrestling fans recognize Garett for the time that he spent in TNA, and since then, we've done a lot of independent shows together and things of that nature. Consequently, his name often comes up when talking about my career in wrestling, but my daughter, on the other hand, prefers a lower profile.

In her own way, however, Montanna has *also* followed in my footsteps. She has been in the television production business now for about a decade, having first started working with Jason Hervey and I at BHE. She went on to become Director of Development at *Shed Media*, a division of Warner Television, creating her own television show ideas – and developing them for production.

Interestingly enough, Montanna was very much involved in getting the *Rhodes to the Top* reality series – featuring Cody and Brandi Rhodes – sold to TNT. Not only did she develop the initial concept, she was also responsible for finding the right showrunner – and the series did very, very well.

'Tanna is more creative than I've ever been – and she's got a much greater eye for detail. She has amazing work ethic and discipline, and she's an incredibly talented young woman that I couldn't be prouder of.

This book would not have been published without Conrad Thompson. When I look back at over the past five or six years, there's been no-one more instrumental in my life.

Conrad has changed my life in so many positive ways. He is an exceptionally intelligent person with great instincts – but above all else, he's a great human being. It's been a pleasure to work with him – but not only with him alone. Getting to know his friends and his family has been a pleasure, too. Loree and I have vacationed with Conrad and Megan – and Conrad's parents – and thoroughly enjoyed the experience. We were made to feel like part of the family.

For all that, I'm very, very *grateful*.

Guy Evans would like to thank:

My wife, Aysha, for everything you do for our family.

My incredible boys: Nicky and Matthew.

Mark Curi and Neal Pruitt for your feedback and input on the project.

Finally, you – the reader!

Thanks for checking out *Grateful*!

Also by Eric Bischoff
Controversy Creates Cash

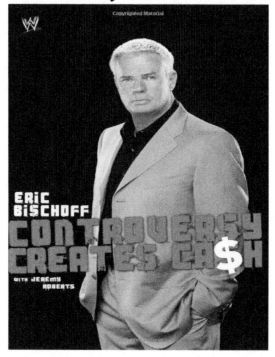

Publisher: World Wrestling Entertainment (ISBN-10: 1416528547, ISBN-13: 978-1416528548)

Print Length: 400 pages

Format: Paperback, Hardcover, E-book (Amazon Kindle)

For more: EricBischoff.com / @Ebischoff

Also by Guy Evans
NITRO: The Incredible Rise and Inevitable Collapse of Ted Turner's WCW

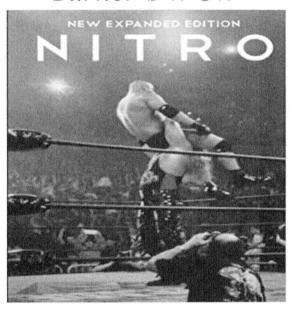

Publisher: WCWNitroBook.com (ISBN-10: 0692139176, ISBN-13: 978-0692139172). Print Length: 590 pages

Format: Paperback, Hardcover, E-book (Amazon Kindle), Audiobook (Audible)

For more: WCWNitroBook.com / guyevanswcwbook@gmail.com

Printed in Great Britain
by Amazon

31210690R00155